Easy Peasy PUPPY Squeezy

YOUR SIMPLE STEP-BY-STEP GUIDE TO
RAISING AND TRAINING A HAPPY PUPPY

# Easy Peasy PUPPY Squeezy

# STEVE MANN

### & Martin Roach

BLINK
bringing you closer

Published by Blink Publishing
2.25, The Plaza,
535 Kings Road,
Chelsea Harbour,
London, SW10 0SZ

www.blinkpublishing.co.uk

facebook.com/blinkpublishing
twitter.com/blinkpublishing

Trade paperback – 978-1-788-701-60-0
Ebook – 978-1-788-701-61-7

A CIP catalogue of this book is available from the British Library.

Typeset by Envy Design Ltd
All illustrations © Shutterstock
Printed and bound in Great Britain by Clays Ltd, Elcograf S.p.A.

7 9 10 8 6

Blink Publishing is an imprint of Bonnier Books UK
www.bonnierbooks.co.uk

*To Gina, Luke and all who*
*work with rescue dogs*

# CONTENTS

ABOUT THE AUTHOR 1

A QUICK GUIDE 3

INTRODUCTION: MY BACKSTORY 5

CHAPTER 1: **MY TRAINING PHILOSOPHY** 13

CHAPTER 2: **SO, YOU'RE GETTING A PUPPY?!** 25

CHAPTER 3: **20 & ½ THINGS YOUR PUPPY WANTS YOU TO KNOW** 45

CHAPTER 4: **TOILET TRAINING** 51

CHAPTER 5: **BODY LANGUAGE** 65

CHAPTER 6: **SIT** 81

CHAPTER 7: **MOUTH MANNERS** 97

CHAPTER 8:    SOCIALISATION                          111

CHAPTER 9:    DOG PARK ETIQUETTE                     131

CHAPTER 10:   PLAY-AWAY                              143

CHAPTER 11:   JUMPING UP                             153

CHAPTER 12:   REFLEX TO NAME (RTN)                   167

CHAPTER 13:   EYE CONTACT                            175

CHAPTER 14:   LOOSE LEAD WALKING                     185

CHAPTER 15:   RECALL                                 197

CHAPTER 16:   NOSE TARGET                            209

CHAPTER 17:   THE TROUBLE WITH
              'LEAVE'                                215

CHAPTER 18:   THE RUCKSACK WALK                      229

CHAPTER 19:   PUPPY SCHOOL, GROUP
              CLASSES AND VETS, OH MY!               247


GOODBYE, AND GOOD LUCK                               253

ACKNOWLEDGEMENTS                                     255

INDEX                                                259

# ABOUT THE
# AUTHOR

IN 30 YEARS as a professional dog trainer, Steve Mann has worked with over 100,000 dogs in many diverse and varied environments – in the security and detection field, for the TV and film industries, as a higher education lecturer on Animal Behaviour and Husbandry, as well as with a number of international sports stars and high-profile celebrity dog owners. He has made many television appearances as a dog behaviour expert, including as the winning trainer on BBC's *The Underdog Show*. Steve is the founder of the Institute of Modern Dog Trainers, the leading body for trainers and behaviourists worldwide.

With a passion for ethical and science-based dog training, Steve has taught throughout Europe, South

America, Africa and the Middle East to lead the way in modern, positive dog training. Steve's approach is based in sound behavioural research as opposed to dog training 'myths' and hearsay.

Steve is also a passionate champion and supporter of dogs in rescue: 'If we get it right with our puppies and educate society as to how to live "right" with our canines, then my dream of no dogs in rescue centres may just become a reality.'

Steve lives in Hertfordshire with his wife Gina, son Luke and seven (yes, seven!) dogs: Nancy – chihuahua mix; Pablo – Staffordshire bull terrier; Ash – German shepherd; Pele – greyhound; Spider – whippet; Summer – lurcher; Carlos Fandangos of the West – Malinois.

# A QUICK GUIDE

If you're struggling for time and just need the puppy training shortcuts ... skip to page 49.

# MY BACKSTORY

THEY USED TO call me 'the freaky dog boy'. I grew up in Waltham Abbey in Essex in the 1970s and 1980s; then there were always a couple of dogs out playing with the kids in the street and I just loved 'em! That's how it was back then. Dogs were just out and about, doing their thing. Yet, at home we never had a dog. My mum tried to fob me off with, 'How about a rabbit, Stephen?' to which I'd reply, 'Well, no, it ain't a dog, Mum, is it?!' So, we never had a dog and rightly so, because my parents worked hard and while it was a lovely idea for a kid growing up, it wasn't the right thing to do.

My family are all Irish, so we would go to Ireland in the summer holidays and over there it seemed standard that everyone had dogs. I can still remember that magical, summer holiday feeling, travelling to Ireland all excited, then seeing and being around loads of dogs when we got there... which made it all the more frustrating that we never had a dog when we got back home. Not being able to have one just magnified my obsession with them because they felt a lot more precious. So, I played with the dogs in the streets by my house to get my fix. Pretty quickly I was just obsessively into dogs.

Then, one day I found out there was a dog training class nearby, so I went along and just sat at the back, watching the trainers and the owners, but mostly the dogs. Over time I started taking neighbours' dogs to the training class. Sometimes I'd even take a dog off the street and go to the class with them. If there weren't any dogs around to take with me, I'd still go without a dog. The freaky dog boy, sitting at the back.

I soon started helping the trainers tidy up at the end of class, then I began to set everything up with them at the start of the lesson. I'd be making the tea, putting up the jumps, getting out the toys, then I'd go and do the same at another dog school, then another school and so on. I became a dog training groupie.

Perhaps, inevitably, the trainers began asking me to help in the class itself. Maybe watching a certain dog who needed a little reassurance or whatever. I got under the wing of a few these of trainers and they tried showing me how to train dogs. The universal philosophy was pretty much, 'Dog does something good, you give them something good, namely a pat on the head; dog does something bad, you give them something bad', which meant you pulled on the lead or shouted at them or even, bizarrely, threw water at them. And, yes, some of the trainers and owners would hit the dogs.

That's when it got serious for me.

I was only twelve or thirteen at this point, but I felt very uncomfortable with some of the training that was going on. Back then, the methodology was pretty old school: at best strict, at worst very harsh. It was heavy handed, it was physical. There was widespread use of punishment. That's how it used to be, but I just didn't agree. There was a real emphasis on corrections – on punishing a dog – and a strict focus on how to *stop* the dog doing something. I would sit there and watch while shuffling uncomfortably in my seat, thinking, *Why don't we just focus on what we do want, rather than only looking for the 'bad'?* The more I was seeing and learning, the more I was thinking, *This training ain't actually very good.*

That's the stuff that would keep me awake at night because I couldn't understand or agree with so much of it. Subconsciously I began to read dogs' body language (which was never even mentioned at any of these classes) and how the dogs exhibited their feelings and what sort of relationships they had with their owners. Behind the very rigid classes, I started seeing the scabby bits: the dog getting a bit stressed but no one noticing, the dog that was scared because of the punishments, the puppy that was struggling for breath every time their owner yanked their lead as discipline and, crucially, I'd notice the owners who were getting stressed, too.

Looking back, that approach was pretty grotty, but it was across the board. Everyone seemed to do it like that.

But they were wrong. I know now that they were wrong.

Those early years were a time of great contrast for me. I was troubled by what I was seeing but also very excited by the idea of training dogs as a job. The problem was, it wasn't a job back then. These dog training classes were run by part-timers on an evening. Back in those days, a lot of the trainers were from a military background or had had a career in the Services; they weren't being nasty or harsh on purpose, it was just the environment they were in. To be fair, the people that ran dog training clubs were hobbyists, enthusiasts, mostly people doing it out of the kindness of their own hearts and, for some, on that Thursday night they were the king or queen of the village hall. Some were volunteers, some may have covered their expenses, but none of them were full-time, earning-a-living dog trainers.

Perhaps inevitably, I started doing my own little bits of training, at first just one-on-one with neighbours' dogs, mostly in the street or a garden. Neighbours had maybe seen me in class and noticed how passionate I was, and so it was a natural progression really. I didn't sit down and figure out my own philosophy of how to train and (more importantly) *treat* dogs; I just did what I felt was natural. Why would I ever want to hurt my friend? Over time people started coming to me for advice and asking for my help with a certain problem their dog was having, and that's how it evolved. Over the course of my mid-to-late teens, it just organically grew. There was no grand career path, I just wanted to be around dogs and, if I was lucky, they wanted to be around me too.

As well as no dog, we never had a phone in our house either (I know, I know, I can almost hear you playing your violins for me!), so on a Friday night I used to have to go down a couple of blocks and ring my football manager from the phone box to find out where to meet for the game that weekend. On the way, I'd often see one of the local dogs, a fairly big crossbreed called Yorkie. I always said, 'Hi' to Yorkie, he was a cracking dog; however, on this one particular night, I saw Yorkie over by a hedge so I went to say hello to him... And he just done me, he flew at me and bit me deeply in several places all over my body and hurt me really quite badly. Luckily, I got myself into the phone box – back in the day when they had a door on them, thank God – and I was able to wait till he calmed down and went off. I managed to get home and was taken straight to hospital, so it was a bad incident.

Then I found out that Yorkie had been put down. I was devastated. I felt so awful.

I couldn't understand why he had gone for me that time when at all the hundreds of other meetings we'd had a good play and got on great. As a professional dog trainer, I now know that he was doing what is called 'resource guarding', namely he had found a discarded sandwich in the hedge, he perceived me as a threat to that source of food and his survival instinct told him to protect that meal. Makes perfect sense now, but at the time I was just gutted, and it made me even more determined to learn why and how dogs behaved a certain way, how I could be involved in that and how I could stop incidents like the one with Yorkie happening again.

My obsession with dogs just grew and grew. I had a few of what my mum would call 'proper jobs', but I was always training dogs in my every spare minute. By then, of course, I was pretty experienced, so at the age of 21, I decided it was all-or-nothing – go for it, be a dog trainer! Bear with me here – remember I was the 'Freaky Dog Boy'. Me deciding to become a dog trainer is the same as a 'normal' person deciding to become an astronaut, rock star or superhero! I set up some classes and they went well; then I set up some more and before I knew it I was lucky enough to have a flourishing dog training business. It grew pretty rapidly and soon I was asked to help with rescue centres, security dogs, detection dogs and, of course, puppies. I started lecturing on Animal Husbandry and Behaviour at the local Further Education college. I assisted with cruelty problems both here and overseas. I never just wanted to teach these dogs how to do 'x, y and z', I also wanted to teach the owners to understand the training *from the dog's perspective*. That led me to study the science of animal behaviour, learning theories, and to dig much deeper into the entire psychology of the subject.

As I write this book, my dog training business – the Institute of Modern Dog Trainers – is a fully accredited and registered learning centre providing education and support for dog trainers and behaviourists. We welcome over 4,000 attendees to our courses and seminars each year; we lecture on dog behaviour all over the world; and have a global army of accredited trainers and behaviourists to help me 'fight the good fight', to promote positive, ethical and science-based dog training to the public. I'm proud to say it is one of the biggest and most successful bodies of its kind in the world.

Consequently, over the years, since kicking about in

the street with those local dogs, I've been involved in the training of tens of thousands of puppies. Along the way, I have evolved my own approach in regard to puppies, and in this book I will try to pass that on to you. Hopefully, some of my knowledge will prove useful as you embark on a journey with your own new family member (and they are a new family member, make no mistake about that). Hopefully this book will teach you how to train your wonderful puppy, but most of all, I hope it will show you how to have a lasting, fulfilling and mutually rewarding relationship for many years to come.

But hey, what do I know... I'm just the freaky dog boy, right?

## CHAPTER 1

# MY TRAINING PHILOSOPHY

'Nothing taught by force stays in the soul.'
– ~~PLUTO~~ PLATO

So, here's the part where I tell you about my training philosophy. I guess I always look at life from the dog's perspective. If I were your puppy, how would I want to be trained? I'd want to feel safe, valued and loved. I'd want to feel pure happiness when I see you.

As I said in the Introduction, dog training for me has never been a hobby, more a 24/7 obsession. I think it's an absolute obligation of all owners to show puppy how to live safely and happily with us through positive training. Training is not about fancy tricks to impress our friends; it's a way to *enhance* everyone's life. Having a dog in your family is a real honour, and doing positive dog training is the honourable thing. Your puppy is a family member and it's a big investment – I'm not talking about the money, but the emotional investment: a puppy will dictate the clothes that you wear, the car that you drive, your next house, your holidays, your furniture. They're a massive, *massive* influence on your life.

For training the behaviours you want, I'm going to show you the very best way to teach puppy so they stay super-keen to learn and get it right. For the cheeky pup behaviours we'll want less of, such as nipping and chewing, I'm going to teach you the methods to get puppy back on track without the use of fear or you having your ear bent by the local pseudo-expert down the park who mistakenly tells you that your puppy is trying to be 'dominant' over you. Yes, I have a big emphasis on ethical and science-based training, but on the primary level, it's crucial to understand that we are not training rats in a box or mice in a laboratory. The training *has* to go hand in hand with empathy and your relationship with your dog, with an emphasis on how the dog *feels*.

There are really only ever going to be two reasons why your puppy won't do what you've asked:

1. They don't understand what you've asked them to do.

2. They're not motivated enough to do it.

It really is that simple, nothing to do with wolves, pack leaders or bullying. Don't fall for silly breed characteristics such as 'stubborn'. No dog is ever stubborn – that's a foolish concept driven by our ego and pride. Think about it: as if a dog will say, 'I know what you want me to do, I'm motivated for what I may get for completing the behaviour but do you know what? ... I SHAN'T!'

Never in a million years.

The great news is, with my training philosophy everything we teach is rooted in behavioural science. We don't have to summon up mystical 'energies' or leaky hierarchy theories. We can have a great time puppy training *and* apply hang-your-hat-on evidence-based learning theory. You can roll on the floor to play with puppy *and* 'get your geek on' at the same time!

And remember: it's *your* responsibility. Your puppy, your responsibility.

A final point here about timings. People often ask me how long and how many times a day or week they should be doing the training. There are two answers: specific exercises where you and puppy work on something one to one, then little and often is perfect. A few minutes here and a few minutes there are far more profitable than turning into a war of attrition! *However,* also be aware of all those other hundreds of minutes in the day when they are still learning. The few minutes here and there are very constructive, but there are so many opportunities to work on training as each new puppy day unfolds.

## A WORD ABOUT PUNISHMENT

No one is surprised or disappointed when a goldfish swims or when a hamster runs on its wheel. No one rushes to the Internet to google how to stop their rabbit from chewing or their pony from pooping in the stable. No sane parent feels the need to fight their baby for exploring toys with their mouth or putting nappies to good use!

We know what a puppy is, and what a puppy does.

It's no secret. We've been rubbing shoulders with them for tens of thousands of years. If you don't want something that walks like a duck, looks like a duck, sounds like a duck and does all of the natural behaviours a healthy duck does, then don't get a duck!

Same with puppies.

Puppies wee. They vocalise when they're excited and they cry when they're lonely. They chew for pain relief and they chew when there's nothing better on offer for them to do. They love greeting new people so sometimes being social and saying 'Hi' is more important than anything else in the world! What a wonderful way to be!

Puppies grow up to be dogs. And that love of communicating, sniffing, licking and chewing never goes away. Nor should it. After all, it's what makes dogs so special, so let's swim with the tide rather than fight against the current.

Our responsibility is not to say 'No' to puppy, but to guide them so they know:

- *What* to chew

- *How* to say 'Hi'

- *Where* to wee

- *When* to get excited

Our responsibility is to teach them what we *do* want, not to spiral into the murky realm of punishing what we don't want.

Punishment works ... of a fashion ... for a while ... in certain contexts. It's also mean and, if employed, its potency will deteriorate, along with your relationship.

Let me give you an example. A few years back I was 'flashed' by a policeman with his trusty speed gun going 48mph in a 40mph zone at 8am. I know, right? Lewis

Hamilton over here! I duly received a letter in the post a few days later giving me the option of two punishments: a £90 fine and points on my licence or the chance to attend a three-hour speed awareness course. I opted for the latter as my chosen poison.

As 'three-hours-stuck-in-a-room-with-twenty-other-adults-that-also-don't-want-to-be-there-so-they-regress-back-to-tutting-school-kids-swinging-in-their-chairs' go, it was okay. In fact, as a punishment, it had the usual effect.

The American psychologist and behaviourist B.F. Skinner would say that the characteristic of a punishment is that when it's delivered to the 'culprit' as a consequence to a particular behaviour, it makes that particular behaviour less likely to occur again in the future.

Tick.

I *did* keep my eye on my speedometer for the next week or so to ensure I didn't speed.

Then, dear Reader, I lapsed.

The punishment wore off.

Admittedly, I was particularly vigilant when driving at the specific time of 8am in the *specific* area I was initially flashed. I developed a habit of looking out for traffic cops: if I saw one I slowed down, if I didn't, I didn't.

I had linked the punishment to a particular context,

a particular location and a particular person: PC Plod. Away from that particular context, location or person I'd learned I was 'safe'. Eventually the punishment had no effect on my behaviour other than a visceral dread in my gut when I saw the police.

Imagine now the puppy on the receiving end of a 'punishment' for jumping up at the milkman one morning. What may they 'learn' from that event?

1. Potential lesson: bad stuff happens when people come to the door.
   Potential fallout: 'bark' at visitors if they approach the door.

2. Potential lesson: bad stuff happens when approached by men.
   Potential fallout: be wary of men.

3. Potential lesson: bad stuff happens if I jump up when Mum/Dad are here.
   Potential fallout: it's okay to jump up at people when I'm out of reach of Mum/Dad.

On top of all that, when focused on using grotty punishments as a teaching aid, the punishment is only delivered when puppy gets it wrong. Imagine all the opportunities you could have had if you were focused on delivering a *reward* every time puppy *did get it right?*!

Puppies learn the same way as we do. If we carry out a behaviour a particular way and that behaviour triggers a consequence that we enjoy and want more of, we're more likely to do that behaviour again in the future. This book is all about delivering positive reinforcement (aka giving something puppy loves) in exchange for the puppy behaviours we want more of.

In writing and researching this book, I read a lot of articles and watched many videos with titles such as, *How to Punish Your Puppy.* I've not seen any entitled *How to Punish Your Senile Dog* or *Geriatric Dogs That Test Your Leadership and Boundaries.*

If you think it's wrong to shout at, poke, tap, kick or hit (for that's what it is, folks) an old dog, then it's also wrong to do the same to a baby dog.

There are still a lot of trainers and clubs where the attitude is, 'Well, this is how we have always done it, so this is how we will always do it.' There is no evolution there, but the science and understanding of these fantastic animals is expanding all the time and so is my training; it's a constant process of refinement because that's what keeps it interesting. So, no, it is not acceptable to punish a dog in those ways.

Abraham Lincoln, who admittedly never won Crufts, said: 'Violence begins where knowledge ends', and in relation to dog training that is so true. Some people will say, punishment doesn't work. Punishment absolutely does work. Punishment works but it will always come at a heavy cost – you will lose motivation, you will lose trust and you will lose your relationship. Even if punishment works some of the time, is it worth it? If you end up with a dog that doesn't trust you or a dog that doesn't want to come near you? How can that ever be a good thing?

Back to speeding, guess how those clever Dutch are approaching the problem? They've set up a speed camera that actually *adds* funds to the community coffers when a car driving *under* the speed limit goes by! How cool is that?! The drivers are positively reinforced for the correct behaviour, the unwanted behaviour diminishes, drivers love the presence of the camera and there's no conflict. What a beautiful and intelligent solution to combat a problem that punishment itself has never managed to fix. (By the way, that skit earlier about me speeding, was purely for illustrative purposes you understand. I'm a model driver me, hands ten-to-two, mirror-signal-manoeuvre, red triangle in the boot, the lot.)

'Yeah but ...', I hear you say ... what if puppy *does* do the unwanted behaviour, surely I can punish them then?

Read on...

# CONTROL AND MANAGEMENT IS YOUR BEST FRIEND!

Q: *How can you stop your puppy chasing anyone on a bike?*
A: *Don't let your puppy ride a bike.*

Common sense isn't as common as we'd like to think sometimes, but the more common it is when bringing up a puppy, the happier and safer you'll both be. As a trainer I can often be seen scratching my chin and thoughtfully sucking a tooth before coming up with the most elegant of solutions to stop puppy stealing unattended food from the coffee table. Having first designed a cunning system of levers, pulleys and mirrors, even I have to concede that the simple, and therefore the best, solution is *don't leave food unattended on the coffee table.*

'Simplicity is the ultimate sophistication' – the genius Leonardo Da Vinci said that, and do you know what – to this day there are still no reports of LDV's cockapoo stealing any of his sandwiches.

As we progress through this book, we're going to discuss how to prevent puppy from doing all the unwanted behaviours, such as chewing and nipping, as well as how to encourage them to do all the behaviours we do want, including walking nicely on the lead and performing super-fast recalls. You'll be learning all about groovy training techniques such as 'Mutually Exclusive

Behaviours' and 'Positive Reinforcement', but one of the most effective tools you can put into practice straight away is called 'Control and Management'.

Good, old Control and Management suggests that if puppy runs upstairs and pees on your bed, put a child-gate at the bottom of your stairs. If puppy raids your kitchen bin, then put a child-lock on your cupboard door, and if puppy chews your shoelaces, then merely put your shoes away properly out of puppy's reach. (Attention! DO NOT WEAR CROCS, no need to go THAT far.)

'Ah ha!' cry the sceptics, 'but isn't that just avoiding the problem?'

Yes. Yes, it is.

Why look for problems?

Why let puppy practise these unwanted behaviours? Why set up situations for puppy to 'fail', just so you can issue a punishment?

*Control* the environment properly so these unwanted behaviours don't occur and make sure you offer plenty of more acceptable outlets for puppy to partake in.

Many a time at the end of a two-hour puppy home visit consultation, after I've carefully pulled on each intricate thread of each intricate puppy problem behaviour, I will draw up a nice, simple, easy-to-follow training plan with plenty of Control and Management suggestions to ensure that the owners' beautiful homes aren't wrecked by puppies hanging off the curtains, raiding the kitchen bins and peeing on the carpet.

The husband (and yes, it's always the husband!) will glance through the training plan before casually looking up and stating, 'Well, of course, it's just common sense really, isn't it?'

'Yes,' I say. 'Just common sense. That'll be £350 please.'

Then I wink at the puppy, high-five the wife and cartwheel out of the house!

# CHAPTER 2

# SO, YOU'RE GETTING A PUPPY?!

Quick question: you don't mind, do you, if I pop around to yours later to wee on your carpet, bite your nose, drive you nuts with sleep deprivation and raid your bank account? I promise I'll only stay for a dozen years or so. Cool, I'll grab my coat!

None of us are perfect, but failing to plan is planning to fail and all that, so get stuck into this book and together we'll ride the roller coaster of puppy parenthood. Hold tight!

## NEW PUPPY? (EEEEK!) NOW WHAT?! – YOUR ESSENTIAL KIT LIST

Comfort blanket

Den (crate or puppy pen)

Hot water bottle

Bowls

Toys

Chews

Food

Treats

Poo bags

Enzymatic cleaner

Collar

Dog tag

Comfortable harness

Lead

## Comfort Blanket

This is not just ANY old blanket, oh no!

This is a nice, soft, comfortable blanket that you're going to take to the breeder a good couple of weeks before you actually bring puppy back home with you. The idea is that this blanket is left in with the puppy to absorb all the lovely familiar smells from puppy's mum, their littermates and their newborn home environment.

Dogs are so governed by their sense of smell (known as the olfactory system) that if we can transport that aroma of familiarity and safety back to their new home, it's going to help pup feel much more safe and secure, especially on those first few anxious nights. Remember that first time you were separated from your mum? Perhaps it was your first day at nursery or school, or the first big school trip you went on overnight? Now, imagine that not only were you separated from your mum, but you were also taken by several members of a different species who all wanted to touch you, lift you in the air and show you their teeth (!), then at some point they put you in an unknown metal time machine after which you landed in a totally unfamiliar building crammed full of scary new smells, sounds, sights and textures. You'd be fairly anxious, I reckon.

Therefore, the logic of the blanket is that the more we can splice the old home into the new home by transferring familiar smells, the better. The comfort blanket is such a valuable tool to help blend the old familiar environment into the stark new one. It's very similar to a toddler finding comfort by holding onto their teddy bear during the first day at nursery.

## Den

Soooo important!

Having a den available for your pup is one of the most valuable tools to help keep them safe and, to be honest, your nerves from shredding! The den is a suitably sized dog crate or a puppy pen, both readily available from pet shops or online.

*What a den IS*:

- A safe and secure place that puppy feels awesome about being in.

- A place where great stuff can be discovered, such as chews, a comfortable bed, interactive toys, their comfort blanket.

- A place puppy can happily go into when 100% supervision isn't available, e.g. the designated 'Watcher' (see 'Toilet Training' on page *51*) is on the phone or is busy in another room.

- A place puppy can be in several times throughout the day to build 'alone-time' confidence, which helps prevent future separation issues.

- A place where *only* positive associations are made.

- A tool to employ for accelerated toileting outside. 'Accelerated Toileting' sounds like a round from a Japanese game show! What I mean is, a tool to make the process of toilet training as expedient as possible.

*What a den is NOT*:

- An area to put puppy in as a punishment or time out.

- An area to toilet in.

- An area that may be too hot, too cold or in any way uncomfortable.

- An area that is isolated from the main social 'hub' of the household.

## How to Help Puppy Love Their Den

The den is one of the best bits of kit you can invest your time and money in, in order to make you and your puppy's life as comfortable and stress-free as possible. To repeat myself – it is definitely *not* to be used as a method of punishment or 'time out', rather as a place of comfort and relaxation. Used correctly, a den will become an invaluable tool to stop unwanted behaviours occurring when you can't watch your pup 100% of the time. Therefore, FROM DAY ONE we want to give the den as many positive associations as possible.

If you're lucky enough to get your puppy from a decent and caring breeder, you may even be able to drop your den off to them a couple of weeks before you bring puppy home, to help condition them to the area. At the very least, as soon as puppy comes home with you, help them to discover the wonderful items to be found in their den.

When introducing the den, don't immediately lock

and retain puppy in it. Leave the door open when possible, so puppy doesn't panic about being 'captured' or trapped. With each new positive association, puppy will learn to go and hang out where the good stuff is. Let puppy make the right choice; for puppies, choice builds confidence.

Make the den a place where wonderful things are to be found, complete with awesome chews, a luxury bed, amazing toys, a wonderful comfort blanket and, obviously, a bowl of water.

Next, you should regularly check to see if the Den Wizard has visited. You don't know who the Den Wizard is? You're kidding, right?! Well, the Den Wizard is the most amazing little man that visits when no one's watching and hides all his treasure (a horde that, to be honest, happens to look, smell and taste A LOT like dog treats!) around puppy's den. After the Den Wizard has visited, I like to stand by the entrance of the den and start to whisper to puppy, 'Has the Wizard visited? Oh my, what's if he's been ... has he left any treasure?!' I then let puppy into the den to explore and enjoy the wonderful dopamine rush of discovering the wizard's gold!

*Author's note*: sometimes, when home alone, I search my own house to see if the Office Wizard has been. He never has. I am a 48-year-old man. ☹

## Hot water bottle

Chances are, for every single sleep that puppy has had to date, they've had the opportunity to curl up next to the nice, warm, comforting soft body of Mum or their littermates. Now, obviously you're not taking home the whole litter (if you are, you're reading the wrong book. I'd recommend *Easy Peasy Are You NUTS?!*), so let's try and simulate that comfort as best we can. At bedtime, or constantly in the den, have a warm (but not too hot) water bottle wrapped in their comfort blanket, available for puppy to snuggle up to in times of need.

## Bowls

Safe, washable bowls for food and water. Ensure fresh water is always available for puppy. Consider a non-spill travel bowl for car trips and maybe a portable dog water bottle for journeys to the park or training class.

## Toys

A good variety of toys are an absolute must for puppy to help with exploration, relationship building (with you) and teething. I tell my owners that, 'Puppy has four hours' worth of chewing per day, what would you rather they chew? You, the furniture or an appropriate toy?!' The trick isn't to try and stop them chewing; the trick is to appreciate they *have* to chew – it's natural and necessary, so therefore your challenge is to *divert* that chewing onto the right target: often a toy, such as a stuffed Kong or rope toy. Whatever you choose, you should offer a tactile range of textures, such as fluffy or rubber, a wide variety of shapes and a broad spectrum of colours.

Toys are not just for teething – they can be employed in comforting puppy by cuddling up to them, they can also be employed for you and pup to play together to help build that all-important bond and have good old-fashioned fun sessions together!

## Chews

Build up a good store and variety of chews. A good chew can help puppy relax as well as offering a mutually benefitting alternative to the furniture! Avoid chews that can splinter or would be potentially dangerous if ingested.

Appropriate chews include:

- Interactive rubber feeding toys, such as Kong

- Softer textures, such as rope toys

- Harder textures, such as Nylabone

- Antler horns

- Bull's pizzles (don't ask!)

## Food

Welcome to the biggest minefield of the canine world! One time I was speaking at a large international animal welfare conference in Croatia and during one of the breaks I spotted two delegates nearly coming to blows whilst arguing about the virtues of one canine diet versus another. As each competed to take the nutritional moral high ground, I couldn't help but notice both were drinking coffee and eating doughnuts!

My approach is the same as it is for feeding myself. Personally, I'm drawn to food that is as 'natural' as possible, so I feed my dogs a raw diet as opposed to what I regard as overly processed food. However, this is a hugely controversial and much-debated topic for another book, so for now I just want to point out that much of it is simple common sense: avoid the bad stuff and make sure puppy gets the right nutrients by avoiding unhealthy colourings, sugars, additives and preservatives.

Puppies generally get fed three to four times a day initially, so try and use a good percentage of that daily food constructively, either to give a good association with the den, to reinforce correct toilet habits (see 'Toilet Training' on page 51) or to stuff in an interactive feeder to allow for relaxing and legal (!) chewing.

## Treats

You can never have enough treats!

We're going to be using treats for several purposes such as *reinforcing* the behaviours we love (Sit, Recall, Eye Contact, etc) as well as to give a nice, positive association to the things in the world we want puppy to be happy and confident around (kids, cars, visitors, weird noises, strange textures, etc).

Therefore, it is essential that you always have a nice supply of good treats to hand, such as chicken, cheese, hot dogs. Of course, we don't want to be using too much of anything that may be unhealthy but a little bit of *Oh my days, that was DELICIOUS!* is really going to help puppy remember (and therefore repeat) the great behaviours they did to get that little bit of 'awesome'!

Chances are, you may well be able to use part of puppy's normal daily food allowance for such purposes (even if they are raw fed). For example, using it constructively in a stuffed Kong to help with 'settle-time' in their den or with the family in front of the TV.

It's important to use rewards that are enjoyable for puppy, so as a general rule use the best toys, games and treats you can lay your hands on. Specifically regarding treats, try to avoid any that have a high level of sugars, salts or tons of complicated-sounding additives and preservatives. The less ingredients the better, so I'm a fan of sliced chicken or ham to get the best results without compromising motivation or quality of diet.

We use food a lot in puppy training to reinforce the behaviour we want more of, and throughout socialisation to give a positive association to places and people. And before anyone complains that I am encouraging obesity in dogs, I must point out that over time we gradually fade out the treats as the training and positive associations become more reliable. Don't be mean when training puppy though, none of us want to work for nothing!

## Poo Bags

Do your bit for the environment, go for biodegradable poo bags or nappy sacks. The bad news is, you'll need tons of 'em! If puppy isn't immediately toileting outside, especially in new places, don't be alarmed, it's just a confidence thing. As they become more relaxed in new environments, they'll become comfortable and the rest will flow!

## Enzymatic Cleaner

Life isn't perfect so there may be the odd occasion when puppy can't help but go to the toilet on your carpet! With this in mind, get yourself a good, pet-friendly enzymatic cleaning product. 'Back in the day' some people used to recommend vinegar for clearing up puppy urine.

Although vinegar is an alkaline and therefore good for deodorising soiled areas, it's since been found that it can actually encourage some puppies to wee in the areas it's been used in!

## Collar

As soon as possible, get puppy used to wearing a nice, light collar. Nothing too heavy or thick as this could prove irritating and stressful for puppy (remember the first time you were made to wear a ridiculous hat or uncomfortable shoes as a child!?). As with introducing all new things to a puppy, go slow and keep it positive:

1. Sit on the floor with the collar behind your back.

2. Show puppy the collar, give them a treat then put the collar back behind your back.

3. Repeat several times to make the association that the presence of the collar = good things.

4. When you notice that puppy is happy to see the collar (what is known in dog training circles as a 'Positive Conditioned Emotional Response' (see page 222) – in normal language: a happy tail, wiggly body, expectant eyes – then touch it onto puppy's neck, and give them a treat.

5. As step 4, but graduate to gradually placing it loosely onto puppy's neck before treating, then removing before repeating.

6. Fix collar around puppy's neck, play a game, have fun, remove collar, stop the good stuff. Repeat.

7. Gradually increase the duration puppy is wearing the collar until it becomes a permanent fixture.

## Dog Tag

In the UK, the Control of Dogs Order 1992 mandates that any dog in a public place must wear a collar with the name, address and postcode of the owner engraved or written on it. Again, introduce the tag on the collar nice and early. Not too big, remember – they're a puppy, not a Beastie Boy!

## Comfortable Harness

I'm a fan of using a harness rather than a collar for puppy walks. I want you and puppy to enjoy your walk together and for each of you to be as comfortable as possible. In my experience, a harness affords a lot more comfort, control and connection than a collar around the neck. There will inevitably be times that the lead goes tight between puppy and you – when that happens, we want to keep that pressure to a minimum, so I prefer that tension to be spread comfortably over the pup's broad chest and shoulders, rather than to stress the narrow throat area.

Of course, in this book we're going to be teaching puppy to walk nicely on the lead (see page *185*); however that takes training and training takes time. So, for now, let's keep puppy comfortable and safe from day one. Get a comfortable, adjustable harness and fit it well.

## Lead

Much like the collar introduction, start with a light lead so puppy is unaware it's even attached. Once puppy is happily wearing a harness you can then attach the lead and at that moment *make like a party**: treats, games and cuddles! Initially, there is no need for you to hold the lead as long as you're in a safe area, such as your house or garden. If you're lucky, puppy won't even notice the lead trailing behind them. If they do notice, then happy days because pup will make the association that 'being on the lead = good times!'

*During my journey I have learned from some great dog trainers worldwide. When I was younger I worked with an awesome trainer from Belgium called Geert De Bolster. Now, Geert's English wasn't altogether brilliant, although to be fair it was certainly much better than my Belganese! As ever, I didn't lack enthusiasm when working with the dogs, so Geert eventually distilled his instructions for me down to just two:*

1. *'Make like a party'* = *crazily play and have fun with the dog as a reward.*

2. *'Make like a lamp post'* = *shut up and stand still!*

## PUPPY PROOFING THE HOUSE

Don't blame puppy for being nosey!

Their desire to curiously investigate *every* square inch of your home is actually essential for puppy to learn to feel safe and become acclimatised to their new world as quickly as possible.

So, an ounce of precaution is better than a pound of cure! Below are just a few examples of things to be aware of *before* puppy comes home:

 Make sure poisonous plants, such as certain types of lilies or daffodil bulbs, are not accessible in your garden (there are numerous resources and forums online to keep you up-to-date with the latest lists and advice).

 Tidy up, remove or protect all types of *illegal* chew toys, such as remote controls, posh shoes or mobile phones. If you have not tidied these up, removed or protected them, you have hereby ordained them *legal* chew toys. If they are then chewed … it's your fault, not pup's!

- Beware low-hanging table cloths!

- Clear all WMD (Wags of Mass Destruction) targets! A happy puppy tail can wipe out six large wine glasses in less than 2.4 seconds!

- Monitored furniture is furniture; unmonitored furniture is a *legal* chew toy!

- Fence off a pond or any accessible water.

- Make sure all chemicals, such as paint, fertiliser and weedkiller, are well out of reach.

- Make sure all garden fencing is secure.

- Electricity cables ... the list is potentially endless! Make safe anything that you feel could be a potential choke hazard. If it's not safe for your puppy to interact with it, get it out of reach. For safety's sake, we don't leave human babies to crawl around the home unsupervised; the same should apply to puppies.

Take the list above and have a wander around your house and garden with a pad and pen. Do yourself a checklist and make sure you tick each one off to avoid disaster before puppy arrives. *Get it done* – when puppy arrives you'll want to enjoy the process, not constantly be on the lookout for danger.

## THE FIRST NIGHT: GOOD LUCK ALL!

Let's be honest, the first night in a new home is going to be pretty scary for baby pup. They've been ripped from Mum, their brothers and sisters, and the only environment they've ever known. Chances are they've then been put in your scary car for the first time and arrived at a place that is full of new (and therefore potentially frightening) sights, sounds and smells. Contrary to common belief, now is *not* the time for tough love. Now is a time for empathy and establishing security and trust.

If possible, collect puppy in the morning so they have all day to spend with you and become familiar with their new environment and new home before night time. The plan is that puppy (and you!) have a full and positively eventful day so that by the time bedtime comes around, you're both ready to 'hit the sack'! Also, if you collect puppy nice and early in the morning, you'll have all day to show them how cool their new den is.

With this in mind, where do you leave the 'seasoned' blanket wrapped around the hot water bottle? In the den. Where does puppy find all their tasty treats throughout the day? In the den. Where will puppy 'discover' the most comfortable bedding in the house? In the den. And where does puppy get to eat breakfast, lunch and dinner? You guessed it, in the den! Throughout the first day, do *everything* you possibly can to illustrate to puppy that their den is *THE* place to be.

When bedtime comes around, bring the now-familiar den upstairs and set it up next to your bed. One practical observation: make sure puppy's final meal is at least two hours before bedtime so they have the best opportunity to 'empty' when you go out for the final toilet ceremony.

This brings us back to the 'old school' approach of leaving puppy alone for the first night. Really? Think about that – how would you feel if you were pulled as a toddler from the only home you've ever known, taken from your mother and family, and placed in a strange environment full of new sounds, smells and sights. Wouldn't you need a little extra comfort if possible, to get you through the trauma?

Rather than completely isolating puppy from you and keeping them downstairs to cry while you go upstairs (which will lead to a pretty grotty night for both of you, your neighbours, and your neighbours' neighbours!), I suggest for the first few nights you have puppy in the bedroom with you, on the floor in their den. Remember, our plan here is to build a confident, optimistic puppy, and to build trust like that takes patience and time.

Have a few tasty treats and the 'seasoned' blanket in there to comfort puppy and be aware that you may have to drop your hand in every now and then throughout the night to comfort little 'un. Let's be honest, you didn't get a puppy for a quieter life!

A huge advantage in having puppy in the room with you is that you're available to let them outside when they start pacing or whining for a wee. This takes great strength of character on your behalf to haul yourself out of bed, carry puppy down the stairs and stand out on a frosty lawn at 3am on a November's morning but, believe me, it's time well spent. You've avoided puppy practising weeing indoors and you've given yourself an opportunity to reinforce that all-important toileting outside (we will discuss this massive topic in Chapter 4).

In the morning, move the Den back downstairs to its normal position for you and puppy to make use of throughout the day.

After a few days or even weeks, as pup gets more and more comfortable in their den and being around their new family, if desired you can start to place the den further from you and closer to the final location that you will eventually want your family dog to be sleeping in each night.

Don't rush it. Remember, trust takes *time*.

As I write this, I'm sat in the office with Carlos, my 13-year-old Malinois. My soulmate. Sadly, Carlos was diagnosed last week with a heart condition, so we're not going to be together much longer. I'm counting the minutes; he's not. He's still giving off sparks and living life purely for pleasure, not a care in the world.

That's how I've taught him to be from the age of seven weeks.

That's how I want your puppy to be. Living life purely for pleasure, not a care in the world.

I think back to the magical adventures we've shared: catching 'bad guys', searching for drugs, singing along to the radio in the van on our way to the training field, and generally just being with each other. We've covered thousands of miles and made more B&B hosts doubt their own judgement when we've rolled up than I care to remember.

I'm so excited for you.

You and your puppy are going to make your own magical adventures and I want this book to hold your hand and guide you so that, in 13 years' time when *you* look back and ask yourself, *Was it really worth all the poop-picking-sleepless-nights-nose-biting-furniture-replacing-change-your-clothes-AGAIN torment?* (that you will definitely go through), your immediate answer will be the same as mine: 'I wouldn't change it for the world.'

CHAPTER 3

# 20 & ½ THINGS YOUR PUPPY WANTS YOU TO KNOW

1. I'm born with the *potential* to be friendly. Deliberately grow that potential every day by keeping me healthy, safe and optimistic.

2. I am a walking Behaviour Machine! Control my environment so I don't do the wrong behaviours and help me do the ones that pay the best!

3. Be my friend.

4. Each time we are with each other, one of us is training the other!

5. Neither of us are wolves. Please don't confuse my enthusiasm with a desire for world domination. I may want to go on furniture because it's comfy! I may go through doorways before you because I move faster than you and I'm super-curious! You really don't need to eat before me, life's too short!

6. Spend time with me.

7. Keep it simple.

8. Remove suspicion.

9. We're teammates, not opposition.

10. If there is a behaviour that you don't want me to do, please give me a reinforcing alternative behaviour to do, then we'll both be happy.

11. All of my behaviour happens for a reason.

12. There are only two reasons I won't do what you're asking:
    - I don't know what you're asking me to do.
    - I'm not motivated enough to do it.

13. Please learn more about my body language so we can communicate better. How I 'feel' is far more important than what I 'do'.

14. Good, consistent ongoing socialisation helps me cope with your strange 'human' world. I'll need lots of socialisation, but quality is more important than quantity.

15. Make sure I get plenty of quality sleep. When I'm growing my body and brain will need plenty of quiet 'download' time: at 8 weeks I'll need 18–22 hours sleep a day; at 12 weeks, I'll still need around 16 hours of 'shut-eye' a day.

16. Please ensure I have a special safe place. Sometimes, I may need just a little bit of 'me' time. Please show me a nice, comfortable area I can choose to go to for peace and quiet where no one can disturb me.

17. All training is about making both of our lives better.

18. I don't want conflict with you. I need guidance.

19. No dog is ever 'stubborn', and I will not be the first! I will never think, *I know what you want me to do. I really want the potential reinforcement for doing it ... but I shan't!*

20. Please don't feel the need to dominate me, that's not how we *Canis Domesticus* are put together. To be fair, you'll already decide:
    - Where I go
    - Where I sleep
    - When I'll sleep
    - When I eat
    - What I eat
    - Where I'll poop
    - Who I socialise with
    - Pretty much everything I do

How much dominance do you feel you need over me, the little puppy?!

20½. Dogs are so much better than cats.

Hello again!

You guessed it: there are no shortcuts,
you cheeky sausage!

I'm excited for you.

Enjoy the book and never underestimate how
important you are to your puppy.

Back to page 3 you go!

CHAPTER 4

# TOILET TRAINING

'It's not a sweet wee puppy,
it's a wee sweet puppy's wee.'

*Q: What is it men do standing up, ladies do sitting down
and dogs do on three legs?
A: Shake hands!*

Believe it or not, as stated by the American Kennel Club, house soiling is one of the top reasons why dogs lose their homes or end up in shelters. Can you believe that?! It's a good job we're not as intolerant with kids! Remember, *we* invite puppies to come and live in *our* environment. We're the host, they're our guest. It is absolutely our responsibility to hold their paw (metaphorically, we're not a circus!) and guide them through the toilet training process. It's simple, but it's not easy. If you're consistent, it'll be quick but it won't be overnight.

Just remember this: puppies toilet when they feel they need to, and where they feel they have to at that time. As a teacher, guide them with care and repetition to show them the place to toilet that pays the best. If you pay well, as soon as they're able, they'll be toilet trained.

N.B.: no puppy will ever pee or poo in your house 'out of spite' or 'to get their own back on you'. To my knowledge, the only animal that ever did that was David Jones on a third-year school trip in 1985, but that's a story for another time!

## WHY IT HAPPENS

Toileting indoors can happen for a number of reasons:

- 🐾 Full bladder control may take up to 20 weeks (and a full bladder is the hardest type of bladder to control!)

- 🐾 Puppy has not *yet* learned the BEST place to wee and poop.

- 🐾 Submissive urination.

- 🐾 Excitement.

I sometimes get asked why puppies choose to toilet on the carpet more often than on a hard floor. Well, puppies naturally feel the need to go to the toilet on an absorbent surface. We just need to teach them that the best absorbent surface is outside. Admittedly, some dogs that haven't had an opportunity to wee on grass will wee on concrete forever because that's what they have been conditioned to do. But given the choice, most dogs want to wee on an absorbent surface.

## 'IT' HAPPENS

Puppies are like us: they do the behaviour that gets reinforced, so let's make sure this particular behaviour occurs in the right place at the right time, and not in Granny's slipper! A puppy most often wants to go to the toilet:

- First thing in the morning
- After eating
- After waking
- After play
- After a visitor arrives
- After any excitement indoors
- Last thing at night

- If you see puppy sniffing and circling the floor (more on this below)

## Tools You Will Need Before, During and After 'It' Happens

- A poo and pee diary (this is what your life has come to!)

- A den, child-gate or puppy pen

- A keen eye for puppy body language

- Commitment

- Correct enzymatic cleaning products

- Patience and a good few deep breaths! (Although perhaps not when you're cleaning up Number Twos!)

# CREATING THE BEST ENVIRONMENT FOR PUPPY TO SUCCEED

As much as possible until puppy is fully toilet trained, they should be under supervision with a designated 'Watcher', or in their small den area. It is the job of the Watcher to observe puppy like a hawk for any body language signals that are a clue that they need the toilet. Note, however, that they can be unsupervised in their den. Like all of us (I hope!), given the choice, the last place a dog wants to toilet is where they sleep and eat, so the den is the perfect location for those short unsupervised sessions.

There are other things you can do to set up your home and environment to give puppy the very best chance of success. In contrast to some traditional advice, I'm not a fan of putting down newspaper indoors for puppy to wee on. As far as I'm concerned, that's still 'training' and conditioning puppy to wee indoors. Ultimately, we don't want that behaviour in the house regardless of what surface they're on, so let's start as 'wee' mean to go on. Let's help puppy learn that toileting outside is the very BEST thing they could ever do.

So, following my logic above, we're going to limit the opportunities for puppy to make mistakes indoors with the use of the Watcher and the den. So now, you are ready and waiting for 'the signs'.

'But what on earth are the signs that my puppy needs the toilet?' I hear you say. Well, I've listed above the environments or moments when they are most likely to go. There are no hard and fast guaranteed signs but, for example, sniffing and circling the floor is usually a pretty good indication – this action is considered a throwback to when dogs used to check the ground for snakes and also to soften down the grass before they drop their butt to eliminate! Other indicators might include whining, pacing up and down or scratching the door.

Over time you will pick up the signs, and each puppy is different, but be patient, be observant and be prepared to leap into action at any moment! Then, when any of those signs occur, pick up or encourage your puppy outside and then wait ... silently ... and wait ... and wait...

When puppy has gone to the toilet – AND ONLY WHEN THEY HAVE GONE – *it's carnival time!* Treats, fuss, praise, play – the lot! Whatever your puppy loves the most, make sure that they receive it *immediately* after toileting outside, in order to not only reinforce the behaviour, but to reinforce the behaviour *in the right place.*

The lesson here from pup's perspective is:
- Toileting inside = nothing
- Toileting outside = THE BEST STUFF IN THE WORLD!

Who among us isn't prepared to cross their legs a little longer to earn THE BEST STUFF IN THE WORLD!?

So, that's it, simple, right? Well, not always. For example, it is entirely possible (probable!) that there will be many times when you do all of the above perfectly well (read the signs, take puppy outside, etc) and yet they haven't 'splashed their boots' or done the deed.

When this happens (or rather doesn't happen), simply give puppy a quiet five minutes, then take puppy back inside again (with no fuss) and put them back in their den. Then give it another go in 10 minutes. Repeat as necessary and remember, as soon as puppy does 'go' outside ... MAKE LIKE A PARTY!

A key tip at this point: as tempting as it may seem, toileting is one particular behaviour where we want to start the reinforcement process as soon as the behaviour is *complete*, NOT as soon as it starts. If we're a little too trigger-happy with the celebrations before the toileting is fully done, then puppy will 'half-wee', grab the treats from you and then run inside to finish the 'job' on the comfort of your best carpet!

One final *crucial* point here – NEVER punish your dog if they toilet inside. One 'old school' method is to rub the puppy's nose in 'it'. This is disgusting and totally unacceptable. You wouldn't rub a dirty nappy in a toddler's face! Stay patient, calm and understand that they are *learning* how and when to toilet correctly. It is your job to teach them, not punish or scold them when it goes wrong. Be consistent, be disciplined and appreciate your job is to help this baby dog. No matter how valuable your carpet is, I guarantee it will never be as valuable as the life and relationship you'll have with your dog.

# YOUR POO AND PEE DIARY

So, here's the moment that you never thought you'd get to – keeping a diary of your puppy's poo and wee. But there is a very sound logic as to why this is a really helpful tool. After the initial flurry of Number Ones and Twos, over a few weeks you'll start to see a pattern of times that puppy is about to go to the toilet. Keeping a poo and pee diary will help you 'customise' your plan to suit puppy's needs and to highlight the times of day you need to be taking puppy outside. Once you have spotted the patterns, be vigilant – it takes patience and energy, set an alarm on your phone if need be; it's a pain I know, but certainly not as much of a pain as scrubbing a rug!

Talking of scrubbing, if an accident has occurred, use a good enzymatic cleaner and give the area a really good wash. You need to really *thoroughly* clean the area, as dogs will often be drawn back to toilet on areas that they have previously eliminated on (in the past, marking a territory would've been important and part of their survival).

Clean it once and clean it properly.

The above is the best way to help toilet train puppy. However, there are three other noteworthy reasons for puppy still toileting indoors that I should mention.

## TOILETING OVERNIGHT

As I mentioned, puppies won't want to toilet where they eat and sleep (see Den training, page 27); however, those little bladders and bowels can only 'hold on' for a certain level of time, so commit to getting up early at the start of your toilet training regime to limit mistakes as much as possible. Help your pup as much as you can, and know that, if done correctly, you can soon start treating yourself to an extra 10 minutes in your nest each morning as the toilet training develops.

## GREETING WEES

Have you ever been soooo happy to see someone that you've wee'd yourself a little?

Ahem, no, definitely not me either.

Some puppies get so overexcited to see their family or visitors that their little immature urinary sphincters just cannot hold on and they unwittingly wee as they say 'Hello'. Some pups may get so excited that they run around the house in glee, leaving a trail of urine for you to clear up (I once saw a puppy spell the word 'Hi'!). The good news is that as the puppy's sphincter gets stronger with age, the behaviour usually improves. In the meantime, if you have an overly excitable greeter, make sure visitors initially meet the dog outside if possible and keep greetings pleasant and kind, but low key to limit any chance of over-arousal.

## SUBMISSIVE URINATION

Sometimes known as an appeasement behaviour, this is when the puppy may lack confidence or is a little fearful of the human they are being greeted by. As with all of the above, this is a perfectly normal behaviour, and with maturity and a development in confidence the problem will usually disappear over time.

To help accelerate the process, always look to develop the puppy's confidence with people and new environments. In the short term, try these tips:

- Greet puppy in an area where if mistakes do happen, it's not the end of the world – the garden is an obvious suggestion.

- Appreciate it's not the puppy's fault. They genuinely cannot help it.

- As ever, avoid the temptation to tell off or punish as this will only make puppy more frightened and submissive next time, which will exacerbate the problem.

- Keep greetings as gentle as possible. Crouch down, let pup come to you. A tickle under the chin is far more preferable than a big, scary hand reaching over puppy's head.

 Be aware of your own body language: be small, be sideways and be slinky. Don't lean over or stare directly at puppy; instead divert your eyes and face to the side and let puppy set the pace by coming to you.

---

### JARVIS: A Puppy 'Cocker' Poo Pee Case Study

Jarvis, a puppy Cocker, was an amazingly loving little dog. A little too loving it turned out as he had taken to leaving his family a little 'present' behind the sofa on a regular basis. I had been around to his house a couple of weeks earlier to advise on 'all things puppy', including toilet training, so I wanted to drill down into what was missing from the plan.

The whole family were waiting for me, poised and ready to take notes; nothing motivates a family to pull together like an unwanted cocker-poo-or-two! Once again, I went through the process and confirmed everything I had instructed the family to do:

Me: *Jarvis is brought outside to toilet at each opportune time?*

---

Family: *YEP!*

Me: *Jarvis is not left unsupervised in the living room? If you're with him, you're watching for his body language and if you can't be with him, you're making sure he's in his den?*

Family: *Mostly!*

Me: *Okay. Let's aim to change that 'mostly' to a 'Yep' for the next few weeks. Now, make sure when he does toilet outside, that you're there to instantly praise and reinforce the behaviour with squeezy cheese. (Jarvis' favourite!)*

Family: *Check!*

Me: *... and you've never punished Jarvis for toileting inside?*

Dad: *Ah!*

Me: *Ah?*

Dad: *Ah ...*

It turned out that a week previously, when the rest of the family were out, Dad had caught Jarvis pooping on the carpet and had taken it upon himself to shout at Jarvis to tell him off. Adding number two and number two together, poor Jarvis had learned that toileting in front of humans in the living room led to 'bad stuff' happening.

So, what was the information communicated to Jarvis?

*Don't poo indoors where people may find it.*

The solution from Jarvis' point of view? Simple. *Poo behind the sofa!*

Poor old Dad was only doing what he thought made sense, but punishment will never tell the puppy what you *do* want them to do. It will only leave the pup in limbo and, worse still, afraid of Dad. That's no good for anyone. And, besides, I don't know about you, but when I'm afraid, I need the toilet!

After explaining the 'fallout' and negative side effects of shouting at Jarvis, we made sure that Jarvis was supervised properly, that he was heavily rewarded for toileting outside and that under no circumstances was he to be told off for what was, let's face it, human error. In no time at all, hey presto! ... we were back on track.

The moral of the story? We get what we reinforce, and what we punish, well, we may get that too, but behind the sofa!

# CHAPTER 5

# BODY LANGUAGE

'Communication doesn't start when we speak,
it starts when we listen.'

Imagine if your friends ignored what you were saying all the time. You wouldn't want to hang out with them any more and you'd soon give up even trying to communicate with them. You wouldn't remain friends for very long.

We ask a lot of puppies to enter our world and play the game by our rules, and to be fair, they make a bloomin' good job of it. If they didn't, I'd have too much work sorting it all out! We expect – on a daily basis – that they learn what our odd little verbal squeaks mean; the very least we can do is learn to listen when they're 'speaking' to us.

If we're going to raise a puppy to become a well-rounded, happy and safe dog, we need to try our best to become canine body language masters.

No offence, but YOU'RE AN ANIMAL!
We all are.
We *get* body language.
All animals do.

I want you to be able to *read and respond* to your puppy's body language so if they're stressed or afraid, you can recognise their needs and do something to reduce that stress, or to assure them that you've 'got their backs'. If they're happy, I want you to instantly know so you can share their pleasure.

This doesn't just apply to your puppy. I want you to learn to read the body language of all dogs.

If there's another dog down the park that looks uncomfortable, I want you to recognise that so you can ensure puppy gives that dog the space they need. Not 'seeing' that another dog really doesn't want puppy in their face can lead to all sorts of conflict and bad experiences. At best it'll ruin your walk, at worst it could put your socialisation programme back tenfold.

# RULES OF READING BODY LANGUAGE

Not all bodies are created equal! The tail of a relaxed Pomeranian will look very different to the tail of a relaxed Whippet. Therefore, spend time observing the body language of your own puppy when they're relaxed and in a chilled location with not much going on. Only when you know what your puppy's body language looks like in a neutral state, can you then truly take 'measurements' to read when puppy may be getting frightened, over-aroused or fruity!

When reading a dog's body language, it's very important that we also observe and assess the context and environment. Body language – or indeed any attempts at communication for that matter – doesn't happen in a vacuum. By looking at the context, we can decide whether puppy may be panting because they're stressed with the fireworks or whether they may be panting simply because it's a warm day and they've been playing fetch. Puppy may have a raised paw because they feel apprehensive, or they may just be getting ready to 'bat' the other puppy into play! Context is everything.

No *one* part of the body will 100% guarantee that puppy is feeling x, y or z emotion. What we need to do is look at the whole picture – *all* of the body parts *plus* the environment – and then we can make our educated guess and, if need be, act to help puppy out.

In short, it is vitally important for us to notice and respond to puppy's body language. If we don't listen and respond to their subtle signals accordingly, then they may take those appropriate 'words' out of their vocabulary and resort to communicating in CAPS LOCK. That's when aggression occurs.

## COMMON BODY LANGUAGE SIGNALS AND AREAS TO LOOK OUT FOR

### Stretching

As always, consider the context. It may be as simple as a 'morning stretch', particularly for long dogs such as sighthounds. They get up, lean forward to stretch their back legs, lean back to stretch their front legs, elongate their necks, then yawn. Only now are they ready for a gruelling 23¾ hours on the settee! It may be part of a displacement behaviour (see page 77) to say they're not comfortable, or it may be a greeting behaviour. When puppies greet someone they're familiar with, they'll often let out a nice slow stretch in a kind of, 'What's up dude?' expression.

### Yawning

A yawn can be a sign the puppy is feeling a little pressured, perhaps in a situation they're not quite comfortable with. A yawn is sometimes used as an effort to calm others around them or as an effort to seek reassurance from others.

## Scratching

If it looks like a duck, walks like a duck and sounds like a duck, chances are, it's a duck!

Perhaps puppy just has an itch. However, consider the context – it may be a displacement behaviour and they need a little reassurance.

## Eyes

'Windows to the soul' – so much valuable information can be communicated by the eyes.

- **Hard, constant stare**: can be used as a threat.

- **Soft eyes**: nice, almond-shaped eyes suggest puppy is comfortable.

- **Diverting eyes**: turning away from perceived threat, used as a pacifying behaviour.

- **Dilated pupils**: sign of arousal/stress. It may be distress, e.g. *I'm scared for my life because of the thunderstorm*, or it may be 'eustress' (happy stress, excitement, positive arousal), e.g. *Mum's home from shopping oh my, oh my, she's bought the chicken wings, THE CHICKEN WINGS ARE HERE!*

- **Squinty eyes**: often an 'appeasement' behaviour to reduce the need for conflict and to show no ill intent. Again, it's important to consider the context. If puppy is proactively *approaching* another dog and showing 'squinty' eyes, then puppy is demonstrating that they actually want to interact and are showing nice clear communication skills to display friendly intentions. If, however, puppy is showing squinty eyes as they're trying to *get away from* another, over-zealous dog, then you may have to step in to give puppy the space they're asking for.

- **Blinking**: the opposite of 'Hard Constant Stare' as on page 69. Shows a relaxed, non-confrontational state.

- **Whale eye**: this is when we see more of the so-called *sclera* (the white of the eye) than normal. Often rooted in resource guarding, when the puppy orientates their body towards the resource they want to keep but directs their vision towards the perceived 'threat', hence more of the sclera is shown.

## Mouth

- **Relaxed**: a nice, open, relaxed mouth suggests that puppy is comfortable. It's generally good to be able to see puppy's bottom teeth as that tells us that the temporalis and masseter muscles in the puppy's head and jaw are nicely relaxed.

- **Horizontal lip retraction**: if the lips are pulled back (like puppy is trapped in a wind tunnel), that may suggest that puppy is feeling apprehensive or fearful.

- **Vertical lip retraction**: as Darwin says, when the body and facial features are drawn up, that can suggest a 'threat' behaviour. Puppy is saying 'Back away'. This is *not* a time to tell off or discipline your puppy. This is an opportunity to assess the situation and to contact a great dog trainer to draw up a training plan so puppy no longer feels under such pressure in similar situations.

- **Tight, closed mouth**: puppy may be feeling tense. Another sign of tension around the mouth may be when you can see the base of the 'whiskers' (the posh word for whiskers is *vibrissae*, swanky eh?) more than normal, i.e. the pulling forward of the mouth with emphasis in this area.

## The Tail

- **Wagging**: 'But, his tail was wagging...' is a phrase I often hear when people tell me about the time they were bitten by a dog, as if the dog was in the wrong! Simple lesson: a 'waggy' tail does *not* necessarily mean the dog is being friendly. A 'waggy' arm from us doesn't necessarily mean we're waving a cheery 'Goodbye'. Our 'waggy' arm may be shaking an angry fist!

- **Erect**: a tall, upright tail suggests alertness or arousal.

- **Tucked between legs**: puppy is nervous or scared.

- **Helicopter**: a helicopter tail is when puppy moves their tail in a nice, flowing circular movement when making a friendly greeting or anticipating a happy interaction. Sometimes the movement is circular, sometimes it is a very artistic figure of eight!

## Ears

Play the cards you're dealt here. Due to selective breeding, you may have a vizsla puppy with V-shaped ears, a bloodhound puppy (oh my God, shut up, *THE* most squeezy pup of all!) with folded ears, or a bat-eared corgi puppy. Due to the different shapes and sizes of ears, it's important to know your pup's neutral ear carriage – look at the base of the ear, there's lots of information to be had there.

🐾 **Erect**: erect ears suggest alertness. That alertness may be a sign of attentiveness (good) or concern (not so good). So, study the context.

🐾 **Pulled back**: when puppy's ears are drawn back they may be feeling nervous, apprehensive or scared.

🐾 **Pinned back**: very similar to the above but the ears are softly pinned back with a comfortable soft body and relaxed eyes for greeting a good friend.

## Head

🐾 **Head tilt**: sometimes called 'Triangulation' or 'Orientation Reflex'. It's when a puppy all of a sudden tips their head 45 degrees as if to say, 'Scooby Doo?' (The purists out there will tut at me for being anthropomorphic but I don't care, my puppy tells me that's 'quite okay'). The head tilt occurs so puppy can figure out *exactly* where the sound is coming from. Their ears are working as little satellites to figure out distance and orientation, so back in the day when they had to make their own living, they could leap with pin-point accuracy to grab the mouse in the long grass, knowing they'd only get one attempt so they'd need to be accurate.

Nowadays, the orientation reflex is best employed to work out where *exactly* that packet of crisps was just opened!

## Feet

Keep an eye on puppy's feet; they're often overlooked when discussing body language but there's plenty there for us to study.

- **Raised paw**: puppies will often raise a paw as a sign of anticipation, perhaps when you're preparing their meal or about to throw a toy for them to chase. In other situations, it may illustrate a degree of apprehension. Maybe puppy is unsure of another dog that is sniffing them a little too vigorously or a strange visitor to the house. I also sometimes see a dog gently raise their paw when they're trying to figure out a novel or curious situation such as their first sighting of a different species.

## Overall Body

When reading puppy's body language, it's good to look at the overall picture the body is painting as well as all of the individual features detailed above, to help you gain as informed an opinion as possible. There's a lot of similar messages in our own body language, so use that as your first point of reference. For example, consider a friendly human-to-human approach to say 'Hello'. An approach with nice intentions is usually on a crescent: the Approacher walks in on an arc, a curve.

When a dog approaches another dog with friendly intentions, what's the first thing they do? That's right, they sniff butts. By approaching in an arc, the dog's nose arrives right at the Information Centre.

I used to travel to Portugal to watch the beach dogs in the morning as they waited for the fishermen to arrive back with their haul. By measuring the footprints in the sand after a dog-to-dog meeting, I could see that a crescent approach predicted a friendly meet and greet. We do the same. When we meet someone for the first time, we approach on a similar curve, that puts us in the correct position to shake hands. As we shake hands, our body is naturally placed on a friendly angle and you'll notice that some people will actually nod and drop their head in a subservient manner as they say hello, putting even more bends in their body. Bends are good!

If I'm relaxed, friendly and in a comfortable environment, as I stand chatting to you my feet will be at 'ten to two', there'll be a bend in my knee, my hips, shoulders and head will be off to one side, and I won't make continuous eye contact with you for more than a second or two without blinking or diverting my gaze.

Now consider the opposite: imagine I'm going to

approach you with not-so-friendly intentions. Before I even make my approach, my body will be upright, my feet and knees will be parallel, with my hips, shoulders and head all on a straight line. My eye contact will be direct without looking away or blinking every few seconds. My approach will be straight on, direct and, undoubtedly, unnerving!

Same with dogs: straight line approaches, direct 'hard' eyes and nose-to-nose front-on meetings are all red flags.

See, we're not so different after all, are we?

But if we ever meet, let's shake hands, yeah, not the other...

There are other important body language signals that your puppy may present which are worthy of a mention. 'Piloerection' is the technical term for the street phrase of 'Raised Hackles'. This is when the hair stands on the back of the dog's neck or along the spine. It's a sign of arousal that doesn't necessarily mean anything good, it doesn't necessarily mean anything bad. It means the dog is aroused, so check the environment and context to ensure that the arousal doesn't tip over into something less welcome. Some 'experts' in your local park or dog club may claim if the hackles are raised on the dog's neck it means X and if they are raised further down the spine it means Y. These people are lunatics, smile and keep moving!

Another example is 'Rocking Horse', which is when two dogs are running and playing with each other, and we see a nice 'rocking horse' movement in their spine as they run. A movement that's more reminiscent of lambs gambolling than predators hunting is always more favourable in dog-to-dog interaction.

Finally, sometimes you'll see your puppy or other dog bow. Putting the friendly end up and the pointy, bitey end down can often be interpreted as a friendly gesture designed to induce play.

## DISPLACEMENT BEHAVIOURS

A displacement behaviour is a normal canine behaviour that is being displayed out of context. Displacement behaviours often occur when the dog is torn between two conflicting motives, such as 'avoid' and 'approach'. For example, puppy kinda wants to say 'Hi' to an older dog, but they're also kinda scared. You may see a displacement behaviour from puppy, such as grooming themselves or they all of a sudden 'discover' an itch that wasn't there 30 seconds ago! A displacement behaviour buys puppy time to assess the situation a little longer. Remember when you were a kid and you were asked a difficult question by your Maths teacher, you'd sometimes yawn, play with your hair, scratch your head or lean back in your chair? That's displacement behaviour. Common displacement behaviours might include sniffing, scratching, yawning or self-grooming.

## META SIGNALS

When two dogs are playing, remember they're rehearsing pretty hardcore behaviours such as feeding, fighting, flight and sex. Historically it would have been important for wild dogs to practise these behaviours during play so, when the time came, they would be proficient in delivering the behaviours required for the survival of the individual, the group and, ultimately, the species.

Today, of course, those behaviours are thankfully not called upon with the same regularity; however, the 'wiring' is still in there. Meta signals are the body language signs that dogs give off during play that say 'not really'. So, for example, *I'm chasing you to pull you to the ground so I can rip your vital organs out to feed upon them*, says the German shepherd as he pursues the collie, '*...but not really, look at my meta signals of rocking horse movement and my open, relaxed mouth. See, just playing!*'

## A WORD ABOUT STRESS

Note here that 'stress' doesn't always mean something negative. We humans always refer to being 'stressed' as

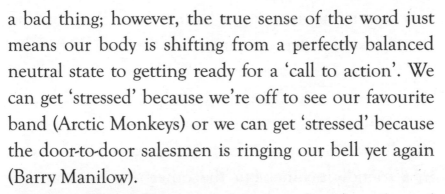

a bad thing; however, the true sense of the word just means our body is shifting from a perfectly balanced neutral state to getting ready for a 'call to action'. We can get 'stressed' because we're off to see our favourite band (Arctic Monkeys) or we can get 'stressed' because the door-to-door salesmen is ringing our bell yet again (Barry Manilow).

Excitement and fear can have similar physiological effects on the body, with a cocktail of hormones being released to activate the sympathetic nervous system. A puppy may display 'stress' body language because they're afraid of thunder or they may display 'stress' body language because you're about to throw their favourite toy for them to chase. For example, let's look at potential signs of stress:

- Tight, closed mouth

- Panting

- Whining

- Ears laid back

- Tongue flicks (darting their tongue out of the front of their mouth)

- Displacement behaviours (see page 77)

If the stress is generated through a potential confrontation, then there will be clear signs. When we mammals are in a threatening mood, our bodies tend to rise up and lean forward. Charles Darwin referred to this in his 1872 work *The Expression of the Emotions in Man and Animals*. If you don't believe me, drive past a nightclub on a Saturday night and look at how the doormen are standing. If puppy is attempting to greet another dog in a friendly manner but the other dog continues to posture up and lean forward over puppy, or they're showing other threatening behaviour, your job is to get puppy out of that situation.

Conversely, when we animals (dogs included) are fearful, our facial expressions and bodies tend to slink down and away from the perceived threat. Trust your gut, remember, we're animals before we're humans.

Being able to read, understand and respond accordingly to your puppy's body language will not only encourage and improve both of your communication skills, it is also guaranteed to help build a stronger bond between you and add to both of your emotional and physical wellbeing.

Like I said at the start of this chapter, communication doesn't start when we speak, it starts when we listen.

## CHAPTER 6

# SIT

### WHAT DOES A SIT LOOK LIKE?

Butt on the floor, (what else could it be?!)

### WHY TEACH A SIT?

You know what, I can't remember the last time I've had to teach an owner the initial stages of teaching a puppy to sit, as it tends to be the bit of 'software' that's already uploaded into pup before I get my trainer's hands on them. However, I do know how often I've had to 'improve' a puppy's 'Sit'. Every Single Time!

It's not just the case of getting a puppy to sit for one second and then that's job done, 'Off to *Britain's Got Talent* we go!' There is much more to a good sit than that. A great, reliable sit is by far one of the most precious exercises you can teach your puppy.

## THE BASIC SIT – PUPPY STEPS OF TRAINING

1. Take a treat and let puppy sniff it. Once engaged, slowly raise the treat a few centimetres up over puppy's head. As soon as the head raises and the bottom BEGINS TO LOWER say 'Good', and give puppy the treat.
Don't be too greedy here, we want puppy to make the incremental steps towards a sit so no need to wait for the bottom to touch the floor at this stage.

2. As above, but say 'Sit' as puppy lowers their bum and delay the 'Good' until puppy's bottom actually touches the floor. Make sure the bottom is still touching the floor when you say 'Good'. If you're too slow, puppy may get back up again before you *mark* the correct behaviour. 'Marking a behaviour' is when you say 'Good' as the behaviour occurs, before reinforcing the behaviour (with a treat). It's important to 'mark' the behaviour so puppy knows exactly what behaviour earned them the good stuff. If they

know what behaviour paid the dividend, then it's easier for them to recognise what behaviour to repeat in future. I tell my clients that marking the behaviour is like taking a snapshot of the behaviour occurring. You then show the puppy the picture and say, 'See what you're doing there, that's why you got the good stuff.'

3. That's it! You have the basic sit. However, there is work still to be done.

     All that's left now is a *lifetime* of increasing the Three Ds: Distraction, Duration and Distance.

## ADDING THE THREE DS TO FUNK IT UP!

As I said above, the sit is one of the most important exercises you can teach your puppy. However, you need to *proof* it in so many locations with so many versions of what is called the Three Ds – distance, distraction and duration – that it really becomes the kind of behaviour that, when cued, *will happen first time*. Note, I want you to give puppy a 'cue' to do a behaviour, rather than a 'command'. As far as I'm concerned, a command should only be given when stood arms akimbo, dressed as Napoleon. A cue is a better word and should be seen as a positive window or opportunity for puppy, rather than you posing a negative ultimatum. So, let's sack 'command', and go with 'cue'.

With this in mind, let me give you an example of the Three Ds specifically in relation to sit – but this idea can be used for so many of the techniques that are in this book. The Three Ds of duration, distraction and distance really are the Holy Trinity.

*Duration*: we may want to ask puppy to sit for 60 seconds, rather than one.

*Distraction*: we may want to ask puppy to sit at the dog groomers, rather than at home.

*Distance*: we may want to ask puppy to sit when they're 20 metres from us, rather than on the lead.

So how does that work in actual training?

## Duration

1. As per the basic three steps, but when puppy's bottom touches the floor, wait one second before you say 'Good' and reinforce.

2. As per the basic three steps, but now wait two seconds, then three, then four, etc. Don't always progress in ever-increasing incremental steps. Keep puppy guessing (and therefore engaged). Sometimes reinforce after three seconds, then four, then one, then five, etc. Learning, for all

of us, is never 'in a straight line', so training shouldn't be either!

## Distraction

1. As per the basic three steps, but get a sit, then put your hand on your head and if puppy remains in a sit, *then* say 'Good' and reinforce.

2. Get a sit and then raise one leg (one of yours!); if puppy remains in a sit, *then* say 'Good' and reinforce.

3. Get a sit, raise one leg, pat your head and if puppy remains in a sit, *then* say 'Good' and reinforce. What we're doing here is teaching puppy that sometimes the environment and 'picture' vary, however we're keeping the common denominator that you saying 'Sit' means they'll be rewarded for popping their butt on the floor, no matter what else is happening around them. This is all part of *proofing* the behaviour which you can read more about later in this chapter.

4. Keep advancing the distractions as your training progresses (once you get to 'When puppy sits, have twelve "cat-juggling" trapeze artists swing overhead as you march around playing the

trombone for 10 minutes and if puppy remains in a sit, *then* say "Good" and reinforce' stage, then stop. You're probably done.)

As with all of the Three Ds, raise your criteria gradually and in wafer-thin increments. If at any stage puppy moves out of the sit before you've said, 'Good', that's fine. That's training. Just lower your criteria to an achievable standard on the next repetition and progress from there. Remember: we're *training*, not testing.

## Distance

Puppy sits, we move a distance away, then we return, say 'Good' and reinforce.

The crowd goes crazy!

1. Have pup on your left-hand side. Cue 'Sit'. When pup sits, leave your left foot where it is and move your right foot a stride away. Count one second and bring your right foot back. If pup is still in a sit position, say 'Good' and reinforce.

2. Do the above, but start with pup on your right-hand side. Keep your right foot stationary and step away with your left foot. If pup is still in a sit position, say 'Good' and reinforce.

3. Time to go for a full step away. Have pup by

your side. Cue 'Sit'. When pup sits, leave your foot closest to puppy where it is and move your furthest foot a stride away. If pup remains in their sit, bring your two feet together so you're now standing a stride away from puppy (if you're now not a stride away, you'll never be the dancer you hoped one day you would be!). Count one second and step back in next to puppy. If pup is still in a sit position say 'Good' and reinforce.

4. As above, but extend to *two* steps away, then three, then four and so on. Vary the incremental stages of progression and sometimes throw in a shorter version to keep puppy focused and engaged.

Vary your starting point as much as possible. Sometimes cue your puppy to sit when they're on your left-hand side, sometimes to your right. Cue them to sit when they're facing you and if you're feeling flash, have a go at getting a sit when puppy's back is to you – if you're successful with that one, then you're heading to Sitting Ninja Level!

When training *any* exercise, if puppy is struggling, drop at least one of your Three Ds. To advance an exercise, increase one of your Three Ds. Only slightly though, don't be greedy!

## PROOFING THE 'SIT'

'He always does it at training class, but he never does it at home' is a common mantra I hear from owners at training classes, and that's because they haven't *proofed* the behaviour. Proofing your training is the way to get fluency and reliability for *all* your cues for *all* occasions.

Don't just practise in one area. To generalise your training and make it as reliable – and therefore as valuable – as possible, you need to practise in as many different locations as you can. Be creative, the only thing holding you back is your imagination!

Make your puppy a *sitting\** machine! (*\*Note to self: spellcheck essential!*) When you're willing to bet £100 hard cash that puppy will sit when you ask, then start transferring the behaviour into more and more realistic scenarios such as: *doorbell rings / you go with puppy to the door (on lead to start with) / you open the door / a visitor is there / you ask puppy to 'Sit' / puppy sits and remains sitting / the visitor steps in and goes down low to say 'Hi' to reinforce the sit at puppy's level* (going down to say 'Hi' at puppy's level is super-important in the early sessions as it takes the desire to jump up out of the equation).

# Sit

Raise the treat and when pup's bottom touches the floor, say 'Good' and reinforce.

Start at the beginning... then add distractions!

# The Rucksack Walk

Introducing the
Rucksack Walk.

Explore together…

'OMG… OMG!'

Pure connection.

# The Rucksack Walk, Out and About

A 15-minute Rucksack Walk will not only help you and puppy connect, it'll bring you to a place us humans rarely get to go.

Make sure you have a 'thing' with you – anything that is safe for puppy to investigate.

Have a Tupperware box handy, containing a new smell...

...and a box containing a new food.

Using all of these things, you get the opportunity to just enjoy spending time with pup, strengthening your bond.

# Safe Swaps

Play with toy A.

'Freeze' toy A, say 'Out', and introduce toy B.

Play with toy B.

# Play

*'Play is the highest form of research'* – Albert Einstein

# Friends, Above All Else

Play is training,
training is play.

# Play Away

Play with sincerity, it's a team game.

# Safety, Connection and Joy

Dogs won't always know what you're saying, but they'll always know how you make them feel.

# TEACHING THE AUTOMATIC SIT – ALL GOOD THINGS COME TO THOSE THAT SIT!

We want puppy to be thinking:

*If in doubt, 'Sit'*

*If I think there's something in it for me, 'Sit'*

*How can I get Dad to give me a treat? Oh yeah, 'Sit'*

*How do I get Granny to say 'Hi' to me? 'SIT!'*

## How to Train the Automatic Sit

Train a sit in the first instance by luring puppy's head up with a treat and when the bottom touches the floor, say 'Good' and deliver a treat.

Get 10 out of 10 as above for a few sessions.

1. Lure as above. A split-second prior to puppy's bottom touching the floor say 'Sit' and when puppy sits, say 'Good' and treat as above.

2. When you can achieve stage (1) perfectly, three times a day for two days, then move on to stage (3).

3. Have five treats. Lure puppy into a sit and give your cue 'Sit', puppy sits, then reinforce by *rolling* the treat along the ground so puppy can run, pick it up then return to you.

As soon as puppy returns to you, ask for a 'Sit', mark with a 'Good' and reinforce as above by rolling the treat.

After a few repetitions, as puppy returns to you just stand still, don't massively change your body position from what puppy has seen previously, but don't ask for a 'Sit'. Here's where puppy needs to get their thinking cap on ... *Why's Mum not rolling food? How do I make her roll food? What made her roll food last time ... Oh yeah!* BOOM! As soon as puppy's bottom touches the floor you say 'GOOD!', roll that food and wait for puppy to run back to you to plant that sweet derrière again!

4. Now it's time to 'take it on the road'. Get other people to do all the stages. When consistently successful, do it in other places. Do it with added distraction. Do it for longer durations (time between puppy sitting and you saying 'Good').

Practise your Automatic Sit in so many locations that puppy has absolutely *no doubt* what behaviour to offer to make the good times roll.

## CASE STUDY: Sit Just Got Real!

I remember one of my training sessions with the England international footballer and all-round good guy, Theo Walcott, and his dog Diesel, a beautiful black German shepherd. Now, Theo had a long list of training desires for Diesel:

1. Don't jump up onto people to say 'Hello'.

2. Don't 'mug' me at feeding time!

3. When playing chase and retrieve, don't grab the tennis ball when the human tries to pick it up, so they can easily throw it again.

4. Make life easier to leave the park, even when playing with other dogs.

Now, cues that were previously (unsuccessfully) being given to Diesel for points 1 to 4 were:

* Don't jump up onto people to say 'Hello'. Cue: 'No'.

* Don't 'mug' me at feeding time! Cue: 'Off'.

* When playing chase and retrieve, don't grab the tennis ball when the human tries to pick it up. Cue: 'Leave it'.

🐾 Make life easier to leave the park, even when playing with other dogs. Cue: 'Come'.

Now, at best that's four different cues that were being given to Diesel which would need a ton of dog training hours to really enable them to be solid. I'll be honest, I'm really not a fan of the cues, 'No', 'Off' or 'Leave it' anyway. None of those three cues tell the dog what you actually *do* want. They're extremely vague requests that make it almost impossible for the dog to figure out what behaviour you want.

When giving a cue to the puppy, always know what the behaviour looks like. Think about a situation when you might instinctively want to say to the dog, 'No', 'Off' or 'Leave it'. Describe the scenario to yourself now.

If it begins with 'I want the dog to *not* ...' then **STOP!**

'Not' doing something is not a behaviour.

🐾 <u>Not</u> jumping up on guests

🐾 <u>Not</u> jumping up to the food bowl

🐾 <u>Not</u> picking up the food

🐾 <u>Not</u> grabbing the ball

🐾 <u>Not</u> running off with other dogs

Anything that begins with 'not' isn't an actual behaviour we can cue.

Why? Because it doesn't pass the Dead Dog Test.

## The Dead Dog Test

If a dead dog can achieve it, then it isn't a behaviour you can cue.

E.g. a dead dog won't jump up on you. A dead dog won't grab the food. (If it does, it's a Zombiedoodle. RUN!)

What I'm saying here is simple: always ask the dog for what you *do* want them to do, not what you *don't* want them to do. It's a much cleaner way to train.

So, back to Theo and Diesel's training dilemmas. I'm all for a simple life, so I will always ask myself or the client:

1. What would this look like if it were simpler?
2. What one exercise will render all other exercises unnecessary?

For this case it's easy – the clue is the title of this chapter! 'SIT'

🐾 Don't jump up onto people to say 'Hello'.
*Cool, teach Diesel that people only say 'Hello' when his bottom is on the floor. Then 'sit' is the behaviour and the subsequent 'Hello' is the reinforcement.*

🐾 Don't 'mug' me at feeding time!
*Cool, ask for a sit when preparing and putting down Diesel's food.*

🐾 When playing chase and retrieve don't jump all over the 'human' when they try to pick the ball up to throw again.
*Ask for a sit before you go to pick up the ball. If Diesel lunges for the ball at the same time as you, then you need to improve your 'sit with duration' (see Three Ds on page 83)*

🐾 Make life easier to leave the park, even when playing with other dogs.
*Get your sit at a distance, go over, pop the lead on and heavily reinforce.*
*Sometimes reinforce the sit by releasing Diesel again with a 'Go play!'. He'll love you forever and*

*he'll learn that sitting doesn't always mean that the dog play ends.*

Of course, with Theo and Diesel this meant that we had to do lots and lots and lots of sits in as many different locations and environments as possible, plus we had to proof those sits with a myriad of distractions, durations and distances. This was a challenge in terms of time because international sports superstars don't have a ton of domestic dog training hours! However, Theo applied himself brilliantly, plus the beauty was that the solution was all based around one basic position: sit.

As the famous martial artist Bruce Lee once said, 'Don't fear the man that has done a thousand kicks; fear the man that has done the same kick a thousand times.'

As Steve Mann, the not-so-famous dog trainer, says, 'Don't trust the pup that has done a thousand exercises, trust the pup that has done one exercise a thousand times.'

# CHAPTER 7

# MOUTH MANNERS

'Biting and Chewing. Owww! So Cute!'

## YOUR PUPPY'S TEETH: A BRIEF HISTORY

Puppy teeth start to break through at approximately two to three weeks of age, during the 'Transitional Stage' of development. A lot goes on during this crucial phase: the ears and eyes begin to open, puppy starts moving away from total mother dependence, then begins to stand and walk by 21 days. As soon as they're mobile, puppy starts looking to explore and gets up to all sorts of mischief with their siblings from thereon in.

Puppy is now at the dawn of learning to play,

investigating the world and even learning to find out what's 'alive or not', and consequently they need those razor-sharp teeth to help with the fact-finding missions.

At this age, puppy doesn't have much strength in their jaw, so the teeth need to be super-sharp to get the desired responses and information from the world. As puppy heads towards 12 weeks of age and the jaw becomes stronger, then those baby teeth begin to be pushed out by the set of 42 adult teeth that are impatiently waiting behind. (18 weeks is the time to start wearing your thickest socks around the house because when you tread on one of those discarded puppy teeth, it makes Lego feel like marshmallows!) So, before we talk about mouth manners just bear in mind there's a lot going on in puppy's mouth.

## MOUTH MANNERS

Play biting, I know, it hurts. I feel your pain, but it's not forever. Play biting is part of your puppy's education; it's an opportunity to learn and therefore an opportunity for you to teach. Hurrah! If puppies *weren't* so damn cute, there's no way we'd forgive them for all of those scars! Well, something has to redress the balance for those little land sharks' teeth digging into our hands, ankles, nose and (*insert delicate body part here*) for the umpteenth time!

Here's how to keep play biting to a minimum. If you have a puppy that loves to play bite, Rule #1 is don't try to handle puppy when they are over-aroused. You'll set everyone up for failure. Arousal inhibits learning. If you pick a up puppy when they don't want to be handled, they may decide to bite you and you may decide to put them down. So, what has puppy just learned? Biting WORKS! Ooops.

When puppy is relaxed, then stroking, gentle play with a toy and hand-feeding awesome treats will all go towards adding more credit to the Puppy's Personal Bank of *Monkey's hands are cool, enjoy them being with you and don't tell them to go away.*

If/when puppy forgets that rule and they put a tooth on any human skin whatsoever, *immediately* say, 'Too bad' and walk away.

It's worth repeating: puppies, like us, learn through consequences to behaviour. As a consequence to biting, we *never* want to give puppy anything bad (EVER) such as shouting, tapping them on the nose, etc, but we can deliver the not-so-cool consequence of stopping/removing 'the good stuff'. In this scenario, *you* are the source of the good stuff. (Congratulations!)

Therefore, the lesson becomes: appropriate interaction = you and the 'good stuff' staying with puppy; inappropriate action (namely biting) = you remove yourself. D'oh!

So, simply remove yourself from the room just for two to three minutes. When you return you can gently start interacting again. A soft plush toy as an attractive third party to bite instead of your hand is a good option at this point!

With enough consistent repetition, puppy will learn to offer the behaviour that pays dividends, and therefore stop offering behaviour (such as biting) that results in the good things disappearing. This needs to be done in a matter-of-fact manner and *never* with any emotion or the attitude of a telling-off.

Don't stress, it's *normal*, it hurts, but it stops.

It won't happen overnight; training is a process, not an event.

Keep the faith.

## CHEWING

Q: *When does a chew toy stop being a chew toy?*
A: *When puppy finds something better to chew!*

There are two reasons why puppies chew: teething and exploration. You need to understand and appreciate both, because simply shouting or chastising puppy for this behaviour will achieve nothing but upset.

## Teething

Have you seen the torment that human babies go through when they're teething? The stress and angst that makes babies cry hour upon hour as they try and cope with 20 baby teeth erupting in their little mouths? Well, *double* that torment and you'll start to appreciate the pressure puppy is under as the 42 adult teeth I mentioned above all start to hustle and build the necessary momentum to evict those no-longer-welcome puppy teeth. This part of their young lives is not a pleasant experience for puppy. And remember, they have no way of telling you how much pain they are in.

Chewing has two benefits to puppy here:

1. It helps alleviate that pressure.

2. It helps persuade the baby teeth to make good their escape.

We call it chewing; a more sympathetic description would be *pain relief*. Chewing ANYTHING is perfectly normal puppy behaviour; when puppies are chewing, it releases all those nice endorphins into the brain to help relax and chill them out, as a stress relief. Some people bite their nails when they are stressed. So, chewing furniture is perfectly normal behaviour. Soz!

## Exploration

Another motivator for puppy to 'chomp the Chesterfield' is exploration. All babies need to explore as much and as soon as possible to become familiar with the big wide world. Us human babies reach out and try to touch everything we can with our hands. Dogs aren't blessed with such apparatus (how strange they'd look if they were!?), so it's the puppy's mouth and teeth that need to knuckle down and explore everything. And I mean *everything*!

## The Chewing Remedy

Our job here is *not* to stop chewing. Accept that puppy has a 'dog-given right' of four hours chewing per day. Your decision is not 'to-chew-or-not-to-chew', but 'to-chew-*what?*'

Therefore, our job is to provide as many *legal* chewing opportunities as possible each day.

| ILLEGAL CHEWING | LEGAL CHEWS |
|---|---|
| Cables | Stuffed Kong |
| Carpet | Rope toy |
| People(!) | Nylabone |
| Table | Safe food chew from pet store |
| Walls | Appropriate toy |
| Stone Roses albums | Barry Manilow albums |

We'll adopt a two-pronged attack: control and management (which you know all about now, see page *22*) and offering an alternative item to chew. In the context of chewing, control and management simply means not providing opportunities for the puppy to practise the unwanted behaviour. For example, *do not* leave puppy alone in an area with *anything* that you do not want chewed:

- If puppy chews the furniture and you weren't watching, it's your fault.

- If puppy chews a cable and you weren't watching, it's your fault.

- If puppy chews the wall and you *were* watching, what *is* wrong with you?!

In a nutshell, do not let puppy practise (and therefore be reinforced) for chewing anything you don't want chewed. If there is a time when you cannot watch puppy, then pop them in their den to see if the Den Wizard has been (if you've forgotten the Den Wizard (already?!) then see page *30*).

Always have a constant supply of freely available legal chew 'outlets'. If puppy has the desire (and the right) to chew, your watertight control and management mixed with the right number of legal alternatives will keep your Jimmy Choos from becoming Jimmy Chews.

# AN ADDITIONAL TOOL: A POSITIVE INTERRUPTER

Believe it or not, sometimes, just sometimes, you may spot puppy doing something you wish they weren't. I know, right?! For example, there'll be times when you're shattered, you've been chasing puppy round all day, it's 8pm and you've just sat down to watch TV and have 10 minutes to yourself. Puppy is on the floor, checking out the room and just as you exhale to relax into the settee, you see them wandering over to the dining room table leg (cue *Jaws* theme tune ... Duuuun dun, duuun dun), puppy has a little sniff of the glorious wooden limb (dun dun dun dun dun dun dun dun...) and then ever so gently they place their little mouth around that table leg for a good old chomp ... DAH DAH DAAA!

Now is *not* the time to jump to attention and tell puppy off.

It's not puppy's fault.

It never is.

A pup's gotta chew what a pup's gotta chew.

Now *is* the time to employ what us dog trainers call a conditioned 'Positive Interrupter'. I hear you saying, 'What on Earth does that mean?'

Don't panic, Mr Mainwaring!

## What on Earth is a Positive Interrupter?

From puppy's perspective, a positive interrupter is a super-special sound that whenever they hear it, they drop whatever they are doing and run straight to the source of the sound because that's where the good times are!

From your perspective, a positive interrupter is a friendly noise that you will make whenever you want puppy to stop what they're doing in order to be directed on to something more constructive and suitable instead.

For example:

1. Puppy goes to chew the furniture.

2. Owner makes positive interrupter sound.

3. Puppy immediately forgets what they're doing and runs to owner.

4. Owner treats puppy and gives them a more suitable toy to chew.

But why is a positive interrupter better than simply saying, 'No' or 'Stop it'? Well, for starters, 'No' as a punishment will not tell puppy what to do. 'No' as a punishment will be associated with you, which is poor for your relationship. It can frighten puppy. It can put us in a bad mood. Plus, we're faaaaar too smart to have to resort to physical or psychological intimidation to stop a little puppy from doing an undesirable behaviour. Surely?

Crucially, if you just say 'No' or 'Stop it!', puppy will learn that when you're not there, the bad punishment won't happen, so *it's fine to chew the furniture in your absence!*

## Making Your Positive Interrupter a Super-Strong Muscle Memory

Choose a sound that is short and succinct. Perhaps a 'kissy-kissy' sound or a word that is difficult to use in anger such as 'yahoo!' or 'yippee!' Then 'pair' that sound a number of times to give it a really strong positive emotional reaction. So how do you do that?

1. Have puppy next to you.

2. Say 'Yippee!' and *within one second* give puppy an amazing treat.

3. Repeat several times, in several locations over several days.

4. With enough correct repetition, puppy will not be able to resist dropping whatever they're doing and running to you whenever they hear that cherished 'P.I.'

5. When conditioning the sound, make sure you say the sound first, *then* produce the treat. We don't want the treat to be in the picture *until* the sound has been made. It's the sound that predicts the treat, not the other way around.

When I look at helping owners with 'puppy problems', sometimes I simply need to address the *symptoms*, sometimes I need to dig a little further and address the *cause*, sometimes both. The symptom is *what* they're doing, the cause is *why* they're doing it.

If, for example, puppy is chewing furniture because of good old-fashioned teething issues, then I address the *symptom* directly – the chewing. I just need to control access to the furniture and offer plenty of cool alternatives to chew.

If, however, after a brief consultation with the owner, I feel puppy is chewing because they simply don't have anything better to do, then I need to address the *cause*. The cause is most likely boredom or a lack of physical and mental outlets throughout the day. We don't tackle the chewing head-on, we take a more holistic approach and build a lifestyle and daily routine that aims to render the cause redundant. That routine will include more regular outlets for puppy each day, such as games, training, sniffing and other cool puppy pursuits (Note to self: spin-off board game idea!) that satisfy puppy's desire for outlets so much that the idea of chewing furniture 'just for kicks' simply becomes extinct.

---

### 🔍 CASE STUDY: Try Dijon for Size

Around 20 years ago I was called out to do a house visit in Tottenham to help a man whose Border collie puppy was, in his own words, 'eating the bleedin' house!' When I got there the gent greeted me at the front door with a big grin and said, 'Ah, you must be the dog trainer. No need. I think we've sorted it!'

No, dear Reader, they had not 'sorted it'.

What they *had* done, however, was cover the vast majority of their walls and furniture in mustard. Mustard! The smell was overpowering, it made my eyes water. I swear, it looked like Colonel Mustard had been battered to death with a jar of mustard in the Mustard Room! Cue the inevitable 'my mate reckons' source of this approach.

*Dog owner*: 'My mate down the park that knows about dogs told me to give mustard a go.'

*Me*: 'Well, he may "know about dogs" but he doesn't know much about interior design, does he?!'

---

After agreeing to wipe off all the mustard, here's what we did:

1. *Mental and physical outlets*: we agreed a plan that his Border collie puppy got sufficient and regular mental and physical outlets throughout the day to ensure that the chewing wasn't out of pure boredom. These outlets came in the form of regular exploratory walks, search games in the garden for treats and toys, short training sessions in the garden, and 'interactive' feeding toys such as stuffed Kongs to offer legal, safe and constructive chewing opportunities.

2. *Control and management*: ensure a plan was in place that when the puppy was at home, they were either being supervised by someone in the household or, if that wasn't possible, they were in their den, which we taught pup was a fantastic place to relax in.

3. *Offer plenty of alternative and legal chew toys*: some pups will favour hard chew textures, such as tough rubber or plastic, and on occasions they may prefer a softer chew

alternative, such as softer rubber or fleece toys. Make sure that chewing is supervised to avoid fractured pieces being ingested and also that a broad variety of textures are offered to accommodate changing needs and the desire for novelty.

The moral of the story: no matter how bad the puppy chewing is, mustard is *never* the answer!

CHAPTER 8

# SOCIALISATION

As humans, boy, do we ask a lot of dogs when we take them into our world to live in our dens under our rules. The very least we should do is help them feel safe and enjoy this weird planet we now occupy together. A key part of maximising and enjoying this shared experience – for both you and your puppy – is socialisation.

It's a big word but a simple concept. 'Socialisation' is primarily about creating as many varied, positive, safe and enjoyable experiences for your puppy as you can, as soon as possible in their life to build a strong 'social' immunity and to avoid future scary surprises and experiences later in life.

Not only is the well-socialised dog more 'environmentally bombproof' in unusual situations, but it has also been proven over and over again (by studies on military dogs, police dogs, guide dogs, assistance dogs and, yes, pet dogs) that a dog that's experienced diverse socialisation from a young age will be healthier and happier, easier to train and consequently easier to live with.

So, when is the best time to start socialising your puppy? **<u>NOW</u>**!

Believe it or not, at this young age, how puppy *feels* is far more important than what puppy *does*. Sometimes as owners and trainers we can get a little bogged down in teaching good behaviours such as 'Sit' and 'Down', at the expense of focusing our time on helping puppy make good associations to the world around them. So, remember this very important edict: to puppy, being safe is far more important than being obedient.

Of course, throughout this book you'll see all the exercises I'd like you to teach puppy as soon as possible, but your investment in training will go out of the window in times of need unless puppy feels safe and secure. If puppy feels safe, happy and confident in all environments, then the training that sits on top of that is *so* much easier compared to the same experience with an anxious or insecure pup.

Let's not put the cart before the horse.

Prioritise. You've got years to teach fancy dog tricks

(if you really must), but you've only got a few weeks to teach puppy how to be a confident, optimistic adult dog.

*Start now.*

The most valuable, precious period is between 3 and 12 weeks of age. Although socialisation really is a continuous process throughout your dog's life, the potency of positive exposure diminishes day by day as puppy matures.

So, let's backtrack right to the birth. The moment puppy pops out into this world until about two weeks of age is known as the 'Neonatal Stage'. Generally speaking, at this point puppies are just wet, furry slugs! At this stage, around 90% of the time puppy is sleeping, as nearly all their energy is dedicated to growth. The only senses that are up and running are smell, taste and touch. These are required to find Mum for food, warmth and protection. The rest can wait. When I come back, I want to come back as a Neonatal Pup – what a life!

Next up is the 'Transitional Stage', from two to four weeks. Their ears and eyes begin to open, by 15 days they can stand and a week later they are walking (albeit like drunks!). Pups start moving away from total dependence on their mother, play begins and puppy teeth start to come through (see page *101* for more on Teething).

The third part is known as the 'Socialisation Stage',

from 3 to 12 weeks. This consists of initially the 'Primary Socialisation' at the breeders (with Mum, the littermates and all the surroundings), which is around three to five weeks. This is the opportunity for puppy to build positive associations and relationships with littermates and Mum through play and other interactions. Ideally where puppy was born and then initially raised will have had lots of exposure and access to different sights, sounds, textures and smells to kick start the socialisation process.

Thereafter the 'Secondary Socialisation' begins, when they are exposed to everyone and everything both in the new home and the outside world. Chances are, puppy has stayed with the breeder up until the age of seven or eight weeks. By the time you pick up your new puppy to come home with you, they have generally gained a degree of independence away from littermates, while in turn Mum begins to lose motivation to nurse her pups, making it a naturally convenient time for pups to be welcomed into their new home.

As soon as possible, get yourself out and about with puppy to as many different environments as you can and let them learn and experience that the world's okay. This *will not* happen by itself. It takes a little commitment from you but it can, and should, be fun for both of you.

Socialisation is *a matter of urgency* and although I'm

not one for melodrama, it can literally be a matter of life and death. Every day dogs are destroyed for 'behavioural' reasons. The ethics of this are a debate for another day and maybe another book; however, the fact of the matter is, a well-socialised, loved and trained family dog will rarely be put on that dreaded appointment list.

Hopefully you now understand why socialisation is so important and when you should start, so now it's time to discuss 'how'. Exposing your puppy to everything in the world before they're even 12 weeks old is quite a tall order but the good news is, the more you can do, the easier and more beneficial it is for puppy.

There's a lot to do, so let's break our socialisation targets down into two groups: 'Environments' and 'Things'. Environments are just places (which are full of 'Things') and a 'Thing' is what posh trainers call a 'Stimulus'. A stimulus is something that can evoke a reaction. How puppy reacts to these stimuli is dictated by their emotions and how well they have been socialised. For example, a desired reaction from puppy to the sound of a knock on your front door could be a waggy tail in anticipation of a friendly visitor. An undesired reaction from puppy to the sound of a knock on your front door could be a bloodcurdling episode of barking and throwing themselves at the window in the expectancy of a perceived enemy!

So first up, 'Environments'...

# Exposure Table for Environments

(I've left some boxes blank for you to complete with puppy yourself, so grab a pen, put your coat on and get going!)

| Environment | Sights | Sounds | Smells | Textures |
|---|---|---|---|---|
| **Outside the supermarket** | Revolving doors Lorries Trollies | Air brakes People chatting PA System | Diesel Bakery Perfume | Welcome mat Tarmac Low brick wall |
| **School gates** | Children running Ice-cream van | School bell Shouting children Ice-cream van chimes | School bins Ice-cream Exhaust fumes | Astro turf Grass Pavement |
| **Family BBQ** | | | | |
| **Football match** | | | | |
| **Outdoor market** | | | | |
| **Pet store** | | | | |

To close this segment, a quick word on a dog's sense of smell. We can only imagine how puppies experience the world through their noses. We have 5 million olfactory receptors in our nose, but a dog has 220 million! They can smell one part urine to a million parts water. If you walk into a bakery, you will be hit by that lovely smell of warm bread. Yum. However, the pup will go in there and smell flour and water and sugar and perfume and the car that is parked outside and the fumes from the delivery driver and what is on our shoes and a baby's nappy and the cigarettes one customer smoked that morning and on and on and on. There is just a kaleidoscope of smells crashing in on them all the time. Meanwhile, us apes just go in and say, 'Mmmm, doughnuts.' So never overestimate the importance of smell to a puppy's experience and socialisation.

And now 'Things' or 'Stimuli'...

Of course, on top of the obvious 'sights' puppy will see, always account for the additional sounds, smells and textures that are just as important in socialisation, as is the time of day. Exposure needs to happen at night-time, as well as in daylight.

# Exposure Table for Things/Stimuli

| People | | Animals | | Textures | |
|---|---|---|---|---|---|
| Elderly | | Puppies | | Sand | |
| Children | | Dogs | | Water | |
| Loud | | On-lead | | Metal | |
| Quiet | | Off-lead | | Brick | |
| Active (running, playing) | | Passive | | Paper | |
| Passive (seated, reading) | | Active | | Bubble wrap | |
| Nationality | | Male | | Polythene | |
| Clothed/types of dress | | Female | | Wooden | |
| Unclothed/nudity | | Neautered | | Tiled | |
| Teenagers | | Unneutered | | Rubber | |
| Glasses/sunglasses | | Cats | | Smooth | |
| Gender | | Rabbits | | Rough | |
| Uniforms and hats | | Inside | | **Weather** | |
| Day-time | | Outside | | Wind | |
| Night-time | | Chickens | | Rain | |
| **Vehicles** | | Sheep | | Sunny | |
| Cars | | Cows | | Snow | |
| Lorries | | Birds | | Thunder | |
| Buses | | Horses | | Lightening | |
| Trains (overground) | | **Smells** | | Hail | |
| Trains (underground) | | Perfume | | **Heights (with due care)** | |
| Bikes | | Cooking | | | |
| Tricycles | | BBQ | | On wall | |
| Go-carts | | Cigarette smoke | | Above head | |
| Trollies | | Bins | | On bridge | |
| Skateboards | | Bonfires | | Under bridge | |
| Wheelchairs, crutches, sticks | | Traffic | | Looking down to areas | |
| | | Teenagers | | | |

# SOCIALISING YOUR PUPPY TO PEOPLE

Of course, it's really important that puppy feels comfortable around other people, but at the other end of the scale, it's also really important that puppy doesn't run around the park body-slamming every stranger like a hopeful toddler smacking a vending machine!

Use your food wisely, young Jedi.

Set up situations where puppy is around a wide variety of passive people, and if treats are being introduced to the environment, let them come from *you*. Puppy still gets to make the association that *good things happen in the presence of other people*, but retains a focus on you to ensure they're not pawing or jumping at total strangers in the hope of hitting the jackpot.

# THINK BEFORE YOU DO

So, you have a starter list to work on, but before you dive in, remember: *socialisation is a process, not an event*. Everything you do with your puppy at this stage should be an investment in your bond *together*. Puppy needs to trust that you won't put them in a scary situation and if things do get a little heavy, then they need to have faith that you'll look after them, that you've got their back at all times. That will build a sense of security and confidence – we're all happier exploring if we know we've got a good teammate at our side to get us out of bother if needs be.

If you're going on an outing with puppy to the retail park or to hang around the school gates, don't be in a hurry to get too close too soon. Great exposure can be done at a good safe distance. Just let puppy watch and observe, let them hear the sounds and sniff the smells without too much pressure or intensity. You're far better starting at a good, safe distance and gradually decreasing the distance as confidence grows, than you are staying up too close, puppy having a bad experience and you then having to make a retreat. That'll put a cross in the box which may take another 20 repetitions to overcome.

One final word before you zoom off to the park or garden centre: it is very important to remember this one word – choice. For all of us in new situations, choice is very important. If I was in a room on my own and saw a strange package on the floor, I'm going to be far more confident going forward to explore it if I know that at any time I can have the choice to back away. If, on the other hand, as I approach the package I hear the only exit door slam behind me, then I'm going to be more alert and wary, knowing that I have no means of escape if it all gets a little scary.

This lack of an 'escape' route will slow down my

exploration. In puppy terms, this lack of choice will slow down their willingness to explore, which in turn will slow down the socialisation process and, remember, time is of the essence.

How then, can we let puppy know they have a choice?

As much as possible and where safe, avoid having a tight lead or any obvious restrictions on puppy's movements when exploring new environments and things. You can have a long thin line from the puppy's harness to ensure they feel no restraint or restriction. That way they can move at their own pace, slow down, stop or even back away if need be.

To complement this sense of choice, your own very important role here is to always be there for puppy, at their side as they explore. Feel free to drop a treat for puppy if they glance up to you or just to help them overcome a proverbial 'speed-bump' with a new object. Your job is to make the experience pleasurable and to give good associations to this mad world full of crazy new things which we're now introducing them to. However, don't flood puppy with too many treats; we want them to have a decent awareness of the environment around them, to take time to watch, listen and soak it all in. If we're bombarding them with a relentless supply of food then they may be so focused on the taste, smell and movement of the treats that they don't get the full benefit afforded to them to explore and absorb the world around them. Having said that, it is very helpful to use the food to make good associations, to reinforce any great behaviours you want more of in the future and to make each outing as pleasurable and beneficial as possible.

So, on the way home, get yourself an ice cream, you deserve a little reinforcement, too!

The two main tools we're using here to get the most from our socialisation window and to help build a secure and optimistic puppy are 'Desensitisation' and 'Building a Positive Association'.

# DESENSITISATION

Desensitisation is when we expose puppy to a new thing or environment at a nice, safe distance so they don't feel overwhelmed, scared or overexcited. As long as puppy remains unconcerned by the new thing or environment, proximity can be decreased and intensity can be increased to the point where the puppy continues to remain totally unaffected by the exposure. The result of desensitisation means that puppy has no particular emotional response one way or the other to the new thing or environment, it's just 'part of the furniture'. Traffic? Big deal. Bicycles? Like, *whatever*, dude.

As always, the better you are at observing and

reading your puppy's body language, the better your training and interactions are going to be. The trick with desensitisation is that you don't try and rush it. Always look to be working at an intensity that is sufficiently low to ensure puppy is relaxed (what we sometimes refer to in dog training as 'below threshold'). To do this, it's time to pop your 'Body Language Expert' hat on. If you see any of the signs below, then puppy may be under a little too much pressure and it may be time for you to consolidate or back off a little:

- Lip licking – pups may lick their lips in a 'tongue flick out the front of the mouth' style if under pressure

- Wide eyes, dilated pupils

- Excessive panting

- Tail tucked

- Furrowed brow

- Crouched back

- One paw raised

- Vocalising

- Staring at the stimulus and not blinking

🐾 Turning away from the stimulus and deliberately not looking

🐾 Hiding behind your legs

As I said earlier, the above signs of body language only become valuable communication when you listen *and respond* to them.

1. Don't put your puppy under pressure.

2. Take your time, relieve the pressure, move away.

3. The next time you're in a similar environment with puppy, make sure you initially stay at a sufficiently 'safe' distance ('safety' is in the eye of the beholder, so study pup's body language), and begin building a positive association as described below...

## BUILDING A POSITIVE ASSOCIATION

Building a positive association – or 'conditioning' your puppy to like something – has many benefits: it helps puppy feel good about particular situations, it makes your life less stressful and it makes others' lives easier, too. This tool simply means we 'pair' an item or event with something that puppy loves, in order to help them feel positive when presented with a similar situation in the future.

For example: over the next few years, you're definitely going to be taking your puppy to the vets for check-ups.

You can do it the hard way, or the easy way!

If I were you, I'd call in to the vets *tomorrow* and ask if it's okay if you pop in every now and then over the next couple of weeks to give puppy a few treats. If they say, 'Yes', then cool, crack on.

If they say, 'No', also cool, just find another vet and take your business elsewhere.

When you do call in with puppy, make sure you pop your head around the door first *without puppy* to check there's no potentially scary animals (or people!) in the waiting room, or you'll end up conditioning completely the wrong emotional response!

Get to the entrance of the vets, then as soon as you go in the door *treat, treat, treat, treat, treat*; have a little party for a few seconds ... then go outside again.

*No treats outside*, you want puppy to associate the 'good stuff' with being in the vet's building.

Wait a few moments, then head back in again with puppy and as soon as you're in there again, *treat, treat, treat...*

Once you've done this a few times, you'll notice that puppy is keen to go in again. Keep it short and sweet in the first instance, and then as you progress you can stay in the building a little longer and spread the duration between treats out a little more so puppy has longer to take in the environment – the sight of the receptionists, the smells of the meds and disinfectant, the sound of the telephone, the texture of the tiled floor, etc.

You'll start to notice that as soon as you are approaching the building, puppy has a waggy tail and expectant eyes – they are looking for and anticipating the good stuff. Excellent, a *positive association* to the vets has been formed. (N.B. if you have any concerns regarding having your unvaccinated puppy on the vets' floor, just carry pup and go through the same conditioning process, that's no problem at all.)

For each repetition, as long as puppy maintains a happy outlook, desensitise and positively condition more and more of the situations that will be occurring in the future, such as a vet nurse touching puppy's ear, then treat. Vet nurse holds puppy's tail, then treat. This puppy is going to *love* being handled by people in the vets' surgery. Thank Dog!

Using the same process, create a positive association to these situations to build an optimistic puppy:

- 🐾 Going in the den

- 🐾 Going to new places

- 🐾 Groomers

126

- 🐾 Vets

- 🐾 Bath time

- 🐾 Nail clipping

- 🐾 Brushing

- 🐾 Flea treatment

- 🐾 Puppy school

- 🐾 Going in the car

- 🐾 Visitors to the house

- 🐾 Meeting new people

Keep your thinking cap on and be proactive. For any situation you want puppy to feel comfortable and confident in, wisely invest your time (and treats!) in building that positive association. Believe me, a pinch of precaution is so much better than a ton of rehab, scratches, crying and fear!

## COUNTER-CONDITIONING

Counter-conditioning is when we pair something fantastic, like treats, with a situation puppy has previously felt uncomfortable with; for example, puppy has previously been scared when they heard your landline ring. The counter-conditioning process would be: turn the volume down, ring the telephone and as soon as it rings, give puppy a treat. Repeat several times and if successful over time, you'll see evidence of a +CER ('Positive Conditioned Emotional Response', see page *222*) as they wag their tail and look expectantly to you when the phone rings.

## FEAR PERIODS

As a footnote to the socialisation timetable mentioned above, puppies will often go through what's known as a 'Fear Period' between 8–12 weeks of age. In nature, it makes sense for this developmental stage to kick in at around this time. At two months of age the puppies have spent the majority of their lives being super-curious little turbo dogs, which enables them to get as much information from the world in as little time as possible. By eight weeks, Mum will be pretty exhausted, so Mother Nature uploads her own 'emergency software' to keep the puppies safe. What was just so recently *curiosity* now turns into *sensitivity*, *caution* or even *fear*.

Now, when the Fear Period takes hold, should puppy run into any situation that's abnormal, then rather than bounding over to investigate like they would've previously done and/or rely on Mum to get them out of bother, they quick-about-turn and look to run back to safety. The Fear Period acts like an invisible umbilical-bungee-chord that stops puppy from skipping over to the Big Bad Wolf to say 'Hi!' Most pups will do this to a greater or lesser degree, so be aware that during the age of two to three months you may well notice puppy being a little more cautious, a little more sensitive in situations. Sometimes they will bark. It is crucial that during this period you DO NOT PUNISH the barking. Puppy is super-sensitive, so in turn you need to be super-sensitive to puppy's needs and intense development. Just think about it – if you punish puppy when they're fearful, you are simply making the whole experience worse. When you make the experience worse, you will teach puppy that, *When in this environment, bad things happen.* That's essentially the opposite of what we want to teach!

If puppy seems fearful, be considerate:

- Increase the distance.

- Work at a distance that helps pup's body language change from fearful to relaxed.

- Don't punish. That will only confirm to puppy that they were *right* to feel fearful!

- Think: can you use food next time at a reasonable distance to help counter-condition?

- Can you create a similar but less intense version of the scenario in the future to help desensitise?

Throughout the Fear Period, continue with considerate, sympathetic socialisation and watch that body language like a hawk. If pup needs more space, pup needs more space – provide it.

You'll get through this together, you're a team.

CHAPTER 9

# DOG PARK ETIQUETTE

'It's not just a stroll in the park.'

Picture the scene: the sun's shining and you're out with your new puppy, the pair of you are strolling along, checking in and smiling to each other. Heck, even the lead between you is 'smiling', it's so relaxed and slack. You enter the park and when you're safely in and have checked that there are no other dogs around, you ask little 'un to sit, you unclip the lead, good puppy stays seated and looks to you for the 'release'. 'Off you go!' you say and as you do puppy trots a few metres away for a little exploration and a sniff as you begin your walk. As soon as pup sees you walking on, they happily bounce up to you and the pair of you stroll away together, constantly checking in with each other.

Then you spot another dog and owner a hundred metres away, so you crouch down and call pup to you, who enthusiastically runs and nestles their shoulders and butt into you for a cuddle so you can clip the lead onto their harness prior to giving them a treat.

You continue your walk together until you're 20 metres or so away from the other owner and dog, you then ask, 'Is it okay for my puppy to say hello? Will your dog be comfortable with that?' The other owner says, 'Sure, he's good with puppies', then you slowly wander over and the two dogs politely sniff each other's butts, say 'Hello'. Then after a while pup looks to you, you say, 'Thank you' to the other owner and 'Let's go' to your pup and give them a treat as you walk away to continue your lovely walk together.

Ha! Well, we can all dream, can't we?!

Okay, here's an alternative scenario...

Picture the scene: the sun's shining and you're out with your puppy, you've only got 15 minutes to get this done as you've got to pick up the kids. You've not been to this field before, so you stress about where to park and all the time puppy's been whining and barking in the back of the car. When you finally find a place to park, you grab pup from the back of the car, put the lead on and quickly walk to where all the action is!

Puppy stops to sniff but time is precious so you encourage puppy to carry on walking, he had a wee

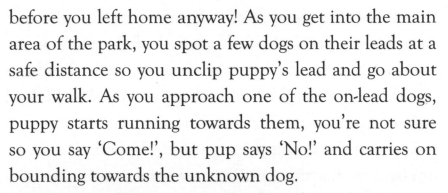

before you left home anyway! As you get into the main area of the park, you spot a few dogs on their leads at a safe distance so you unclip puppy's lead and go about your walk. As you approach one of the on-lead dogs, puppy starts running towards them, you're not sure so you say 'Come!', but pup says 'No!' and carries on bounding towards the unknown dog.

'Can you call your pup back, please?' says the owner at a distance. 'It's okay, he's friendly,' you shout, but deep down you know ... that's not the point, is it?

As pup gets to the other dog, they're instantly flattened and growled at by the adult dog. You run to catch up and arrive just in time to hear puppy scream in fear as another big paw slams into their spine.

What do you say to the owner? What can you say?

It's all a bit too late. Their dog was on the lead, your pup was off-lead, your pup ran up to them and had no recall. You're so upset that you put puppy back on-lead and you march back to the car. On the way back, the lead goes tight as pup tries to squat to go to the toilet. Perfect, you've got no poo bags!

Tomorrow, you go to put puppy in the car for another trip to the park. Guess what? Puppy is now afraid to get into the car because they think, *Yesterday when this sequence of events happened it led to a very frightening and painful experience.*

Example One may be a Canine Holy Grail and Example Two, well, I wouldn't wish that on my worst enemy, but how can we aim to get more of the first and less of the second? Well, first of all, you need to *PLAN*. Failure to plan is planning to fail your pup.

Research shows that we are more likely to remember negative events than neutral or even positive events. From a survival and evolutionary perspective, that makes sense but, as a new puppy owner, it really emphasises that we want to avoid as much as possible the opportunity for puppy to have a bad experience with another dog, child or stranger. One bad experience could really make an unfortunately large withdrawal from puppy's 'confidence account'.

The most important thing we can do as new owners is to build a happy, confident and optimistic puppy. If we have an optimistic puppy that always looks for the good in an environment or situation, then our life with our pup will be so much more relaxed and fun.

So, where do you start? Well, you wouldn't book a party without checking out the venue first. You wouldn't send your child to a school without visiting the school to get a feel for it, find out that it's safe, has no bullies and is a nice, positive environment for learning. Well, your local park also has the potential to be a pretty huge learning establishment for your puppy – don't let it be the school of hard knocks! So, do a recce!

Head out on a fact-finding mission – without pup – to discover appropriate walking, playing and socialisation areas. Here's a few points to consider:

- 🐾 If you are driving to the area, is there plenty of safe space to be able to 'unload' puppy from the car without being ambushed or overwhelmed by dogs and people?

- 🐾 If you are walking to the area, is it close enough? While puppy is growing they should have a limit on the amount of walking to ensure that physically they're not over-stretched. We also don't want pup to be tired by the time they arrive at the park. Tired dogs can be grumpy dogs and we want each visit to be fun and safe.

- 🐾 Does the layout of the area allow for puppy to be able to watch and 'take in' all the new sights and sounds at a safe distance? It's important puppy can experience this new world at their own pace. Too small an area or too close to the new stimuli (dogs, kids, people, bikes, etc) may lead to panic and negative associations.

- 🐾 Do you get a vibe that the park has sensible, appropriate dogs (and owners!)? What we're looking for here is nice, gentle and relaxed dogs. You don't want to be seeing high-octane chase games everywhere and too much rough and tumble from the other dogs.

🐾 Are there some nice quiet areas away from the 'main drag' where you'll be able to sit with puppy for quiet time, perhaps for a Rucksack Session (*a what?* See later in Chapter 18) or just to watch the world go by and to avoid being overwhelmed.

🐾 Is there a more appropriate time to visit? Some parks are quieter at certain times of the day. Initially these quiet times may be the best to visit so puppy can get used to the environment first then, once settled, you can 'upgrade' to the busier periods.

So, you've done the recce, and you've decided on the timing and location of your first outing. Question is, what do you take?

## RECOMMENDED KIT FOR OUTINGS

**Poo bags:** one of the basics! I'd rather you forget to bring your puppy than your poo bags. There's an old military survival mantra: 'Two is one, one is none'. Bring at least three to avoid the, 'Oh, you're kidding me, AGAIN?!' moment.

**Treats**: don't turn up to a gun fight with a knife. Bring the BEST treats you possibly can for your outings with puppy. We're using the treats here for two major investments: to give a good association to the new environments you're introducing puppy to *and* to deliver a great consequence to the behaviours we want more of. Every day's a school day and we never want to miss opportunities to heavily reinforce the behaviours we want more of. The behaviours you're reinforcing here may be the behaviours you've asked for such as a nice recall or a sit, or it may be a behaviour that you spot puppy doing and you'd like to see that repeated in the future, such as toileting outside or checking in with you as you walk together. If you love it, reinforce it!

**Treat pouch**: not only is this a convenient way to carry your treats, poo bags, etc, but it's also a nice visual signal for both you and your puppy to put your 'game faces' on!

**Long line**: want to give puppy a little more 'freedom' to explore but don't want to lose all contact? Sounds sensible – get yourself a nice long line. Dependent on the size of your puppy, a long line can be anything in length between five and ten metres: too short and you'll inadvertently make the line tight and uncomfortable;

too long (or too thick) and it'll be too heavy for puppy to heave around the park!

There are nice options on the market now. Get one without a loop handle as you may evolve to just letting the long line trail behind puppy rather than holding it yourself all the time. You won't want a handle that could potentially get caught on sticks, etc. And note, a long line is *not* a retractable line, this is just a long, single piece of material.

If you live in an area that has plenty of rainfall, consider a biothane line as they don't absorb extra water, and therefore don't absorb extra weight!

**Important note**: a long line is *not* designed to replace good recall training. Also, *do not* use the long line to pull puppy into you. That's uncomfortable for them and it won't create a good positive association for puppy coming to you. If you want puppy to come to you, then you need to give them a positive reason to do that, and this is where your perfect 'Recall' will come in – see later in Chapter 15.

If you do pull puppy on the long line, I will hunt you down, I will find you and I will train you!

## SET UP A DATE

Has puppy already met and got on well with another dog elsewhere? If so, perhaps you could arrange to 'accidently' bump into each other on the first one or two visits to the park. The added familiarity and guaranteed safe meeting will add to pup's confidence and optimism for return visits to the park. The knowledge of a safe and friendly greeting will also add value to your own personal experience of the dog walk.

## ASK FIRST. ALWAYS.

*Better to seek permission than forgiveness.* If you see another owner with their dog at the park and you think the dog may be an appropriate meet-and-greet for puppy, *please* ask from a distance first. *Never* assume that all other dogs will be happy with a puppy running up to them – they won't. The responsibility for your pup's experiences is on you, never the other dog and never the other owner. As much as physically possible, ensure all meetings are positive experiences; if in doubt, walk away. There'll be better opportunities later. Also, it's good practice for puppy to learn that not every single dog is there to be greeted. We don't want to set up an expectation, and therefore a potential frustration, in puppy that every single dog is a guaranteed meet-and-greet. If you constantly let puppy go up to every dog they see, then in the future when such a meet isn't appropriate, puppy will start to get frustrated. Frustration is the fuel behind a lot of unwanted behaviours such as pulling, whining and barking. They need to learn that sometimes other dogs say 'Hello', sometimes they don't. Just like us.

Let's say on average that initially you say 'Hi' to every one in five dogs that you meet. That's a sensible target and will help avoid creating a 'frustrated greeter'.

## AND FINALLY, SOME SIMPLE PARK ETIQUETTE RULES TO OBSERVE

- Pick up poop.

- If another dog is on the lead, *there is a reason they are on a lead*! I repeat: don't let your puppy run up to other dogs unless you've asked if it's okay to do so first.

- Not every dog wants to play with every other dog, no more than you want to lace daisies through the hair of every stranger you pass on the street! It's not sufficient, responsible, safe or fair to shout, 'It's okay, he's friendly!' from 200 metres. Why? We need to be considerate, not just to our own puppy, but also to everyone else at the park. Maybe the other dog doesn't like other dogs. Maybe they're afraid. Maybe the other owner is trying really hard to train their dog and can really do without the 'puppy-ambush' at this time! Maybe the other owner is having a difficult time and really needs some quiet moments alone with their thoughts and their dog. Perhaps the other dog is old or has an injury and really shouldn't risk being pounced upon or getting overexcited. Remember, if the other dog is on a lead, there's definitely a really good reason. Always ask first before you are too close.

- Every day's a school day. Any time spent with your pup, one of you is training the other one! Reinforce what you love and don't allow unwanted behaviour to be practised.

- Let puppy know you've 'got their back'. Don't put puppy in a situation in which they may feel scared. Trust in your relationship is everything. You're a team.

- First impressions last, so make sure all initial introductions are supervised and polite.

- Tomorrow is another day. Don't let play go on too long, don't let puppy become an adrenalin junkie. We want the sight of other dogs and going to the park to be associated with enjoyment and relaxation, *not* an adrenaline-fuelled rollercoaster!

- *Do not* leave pups and dogs to 'sort it out'. Your pup - your responsibility. One bad experience with another dog can shade your puppy's whole life.

- If you're watching your phone, you won't know where your pup is, but if you're watching your puppy, your phone will still be where you left it! *Watch your puppy.*

## CHAPTER 10

# PLAY-AWAY

'Play is the highest form of research.'
**ALBERT EINSTEIN**

Remember your childhood days?
I bet your best friend wasn't necessarily the kid that commanded you do things for them or the one that brought your school dinners to the table. I bet your bestest friend, your BFF (*one for the kids!*), the one that makes you smile when you think back to them was the one you played with the most, the one you chased, the one that chased you, the one you competed with most often to 'win' the game.

Play is the best.

Play is ubiquitous in mammals, especially the young.

It just makes us, and puppies, feel good.

Play can develop the ability to improvise, the ability to be social, the ability to deal with frustration and the ability to develop impulse control. All great skills to furnish puppy with to help them deal with unexpected events later in life.

I recently had to take someone to the emergency room of a hospital and in the waiting room I watched several sick and injured children play with the toys that were provided. *That's* how important play is.

Now, you giving a toy to your puppy to play with on their own gives me no more satisfaction that you telling me that your puppy gets plenty of walks because you leave the back door open!

Play is at its most potent when it's a *social* activity.

Do not expect puppy to play on their own.

I want <u>you</u> to play with puppy – the dividends for puppy are huge and do you know what? You're a mammal: the science says you'll love it too!

So, a few ideas to think about...

## WHAT ACTUALLY *IS* PUPPY PLAY?

Believe it or not, when we're playing with puppy, not only are we helping them develop their social learning skills, capacity to communicate, psychological robustness and a good old-fashioned love of a game, we're helping them to satisfy certain elements of their predatory motor pattern. This is a phrase coined by ethologists (people that study animals in their natural environment) to reflect the 'wiring' inside all dogs that we've either emphasised or supressed through selective breeding, initially for the working and sporting ability of chosen breeds. For example, terriers were bred so they loved to shake-kill their quarry; collies love to eye-stalk their flock/prey, and beagles will follow their nose.

When performed, these selected behaviours intrinsically feel so good to the dog that they want to do more; the more they do, the better they get at them and so the big wheel keeps on turning, generation to generation. The full predatory motor pattern is below:

Track – Eye/Stalk – Chase – Grab/Bite – Shake/ Kill-Bite – Dissect – Eat

Back in the day, imagine our archetypal wild dog who had to make their own living, catch their own protein and provide their own energy source. They needed to feel pretty good about practising all of the elements of the predatory motor pattern, so they could become proficient and effective when the time came. Failure to catch their own protein and energy source would have resulted in the failure of the individual and, ultimately, the failure of the species.

So _that's_ why they like Frisbees!

Let's break that list down into its component parts:

**Tracking**: imagine the dog wandering around the woods whistling to themselves when all of a sudden BOOM, that sweet aroma of a rabbit's footprint caresses the dog's nostrils. Dinner bell. Our dog needs to follow footprint-by-footprint in order to find the source.

**Eye/Stalk**: our dog has now followed their nose up to the point where they've spotted the rabbit with their own eyes. No need to follow the nose from hereon, the hunting baton gets handed over to the eyes. The challenge here is to creep and slink up to the rabbit to get as close as energy-efficiently as possible, without being detected by the quarry.

**Chase**: this is when Brer Rabbit looks up, spots the dog and says, 'Uh, oh!' Pow! Bunny runs for their life. Pow! Hungry dog gives chase.

**Grab/Bite**: if the chase is successful then the dog bites down, grabs the rabbit and holds on for dear life.

**Shake/Kill**: if the grab bite is successful, then the dog shakes their prey.

**Dissect**: if the kill is successful, then the dog dissects the prey.

**Eat**: the predatory wiring has done its job.

Certain breeds and individuals may have a penchant for various elements of that sequence, but it's not guaranteed. Like us, all pups are different. Some of us love nightclubs, some of us can think of nothing worse and that's just fine. Learn to develop play in the way that you and your puppy enjoy the most. I'll describe a few different play strategies later. The key point to remember is to *play the games they love*.

On top of the predatory role-play above, your sessions will deliver:

- Bonding
- Fun
- Physical outlet
- Mental outlet
- Positive associations with you
- Positive associations to the environment you're playing in
- A new 'currency' to use as positive reinforcement to exchange for the behaviours you want more of
- The opportunity to interact with each other in playful, zero-pressure way, which is priceless

What follows are a few options of play to try out. Try them all on for size and eventually the wand will choose the wizard! Before you do, though, get down on your knees and 'prey'!

During play, meet puppies at their own level. Not just from a height perspective, but concentrate on playing with no more strength, speed or activity level than a sibling puppy of the same age would assert. Hold toys with fingertips, not a white-knuckled fist! As far as strategy is concerned, I love being the Useful Idiot in all games, constantly losing my grip of the toy, 'Arghhh, I'm so weak, you're so strong!' as I sprawl and get dragged along the ground by puppy's sheer superhero power!

Do you know why? Because that builds confidence and joy in puppy.

We want to build a love of the game because guess what? You're the source of the game.

Who's the superhero now?

## Tug

Ever been told, 'You shouldn't play tug with your puppy'? Or if you really must, then:

'You should never let puppy win a game of tug with you'?

Be honest, I bet the person that told you that was pretty boring, eh? Probably not the kind of person you'd want to play with anyway! From puppy's perspective, why would they want to play a game that they're never going to win? I'm sure your ego is strong enough that you're happy to let puppy 'win' plenty of times. Imagine being so insecure that you must defeat the puppy opposition at all costs, like some nervy Conan the Barbarian!

Tips on playing tug with your puppy:

- Do it, but be sensible. You're playing with a baby puppy, not a grizzly bear!

- Keep your own body soft, relaxed and compromising to puppy's movements.

- Keep arousal low.

- When arousal gets too high, it limits the ability of puppy to listen. The emphasis shifts from social fun and starts heading towards a more selfish possession and 'killing' motivation. That's not so constructive and adds nothing positive to your relationship.

- Play needs to remain a team game.

- If puppy starts to shake the toy, bites your hands or their pupils get a little dilated then stop the game for a while to allow arousal levels to come down.

If puppy quickly becomes aroused during games of tug, try these tips:

- Only hold the toy by your fingertips; this ensures that not too much tension is put on the 'tug'.

- As soon as puppy 'wins' the toy, encourage them back to you to re-engage. Make sure the fun is focused on the game rather than the possession.

- Make sure that when you're both holding the toy, your hand movements are low and gently moving from side to side.

- Avoid jagged movements with your hands.

- Ensure puppy's feet are always in contact with the ground and not 'dangling' in the air. Lifting the pup will encourage a more determined and desperate bite, plus it puts far too much unwanted pressure on those delicate puppy teeth. (I know they don't feel delicate when they nip you on the nose, but they are!)

- Keep doing lots of swaps of treats for the toy (see 'Safe Swaps' on page 223). This will prevent the game from hitting too high a crescendo, plus it will be a nice foundation for later 'Safe Swaps' training.

🐾 Keep sessions short and taper the arousal level down a few notches towards the end of each session rather than coming to an emergency stop. A lot of trainers will tell you to 'end on a high'. There's a big difference between ending on a 'high' and ending on a good note. End on the latter: don't abruptly leave a 'high' puppy twiddling their thumbs!

## What Hand?

Not all play has to be Chasey, Grabby, Killy and Bitey! (The four evil dwarves they never tell you about!) A nice, simple and rewarding exercise is 'What Hand?' It engages puppy's nose and is a lovely way for puppy to learn that not all play has to be at 100mph.

1. Much like a favourite uncle, sit on the floor and put your two hands behind your back.

2. Place a tasty treat or two in one hand, leaving the other hand empty.

3. Bring your two closed fists around to your front and let puppy sniff each hand.

4. When puppy 'decides' where the goodies are by concentrating their attention on the correct hand, simply say, 'Good!' and open your hand to give puppy their prize.

This is a nice simple exercise for puppy to enjoy some focused nose-work, but it can also offer a relaxed gateway exercise to introduce children to puppy and vice versa. Relaxed, focused and rewarding. If you want to add a bit more energy to the action, when puppy indicates the correct hand, you can flick the treat along the floor for puppy to chase (see, all roads lead back to back to the old predatory motor pattern: chase and grab the treat / chase and grab the squirrel). The bonus here is that as soon as puppy has grabbed and eaten their treat, their next step will be to look and run back to you for another repetition. Puppy automatically running back and checking in with you is going to be a great foundation for future 'Eye Contact' and also 'Recall' training (see pages *175* and *197*).

## PLAY AS A REINFORCER

In addition to food, you now have another currency to exchange for the behaviours you love from pup. You can reinforce puppy automatically running back to you down the park with a great game of tug or have a quiet game of 'What Hand?' as you wait in the vets for puppy's health check.

Ten minutes of play with your puppy will bring you to a wonderful place that adults rarely get to visit nowadays. And remember, for best results, play with *sincerity*.

## CHAPTER 11

# JUMPING UP

## JUMPING UP – WHY?

So exactly why do puppies jump up at people? Because they luuurve you! Let's start with a state-ment of fact: jumping up is a normal behaviour in puppies. It's a natural (and usually reinforced) behaviour for puppy to jump up to the face of their mother to gain attention. Puppies will also naturally target their focus onto Mum's face to lick the commissure (a swanky term for 'corners') of her mouth, which in turn stimulates her to regurgitate food which puppy then eats. Yum. Enjoy your breakfast! It's therefore a natural progression for puppy to jump up at humans who are their new family in search of further attention and reinforcement. The motivation behind jumping up is perfectly normal and natural – we just give it a longer tail by deliberately or inadvertently reinforcing that behaviour.

## THE ISSUE

1. Not everyone appreciates dirty paw prints all over their new outfit just as they're about to head out to the wedding! Who knew?!

2. Some people may be frightened by a dog jumping up at them.

3. Some children may be inadvertently hurt by puppy's claws if they're allowed to jump up on them.

## THE PERSISTENT OFFENDER

As we've seen above, jumping up is a natural behaviour which is reinforced by puppy's mum. However, puppy is no longer with their mum, therefore it's no longer being reinforced, so why does the jumping up persist? Maybe, just maybe, the behaviour *is* still being reinforced?

If puppy jumps up and you (or anyone for that matter) gives puppy some much desired attention, then the behaviour has been reinforced. Behaviour that gets reinforced is more likely to be repeated in the future.

This is a perfect example of the value of consistency in dog training. So, you and your family need to decide here and now on one of the two options below:

1. We do not want puppy to jump on anybody.

2. We want puppy to jump on everybody (including babies, pensioners, police officers, etc).

## LET'S FIX THIS – MUTUALLY EXCLUSIVE BEHAVIOURS

Our job here is to manage the environment so puppy doesn't get reinforced for the now unwanted behaviour and to heavily reinforce a new, alternative behaviour. We'll refer to that new, alternative behaviour as an MEB: 'Mutually Exclusive Behaviour'. If puppy is doing a Mutually Exclusive Behaviour then they cannot be doing the unwanted behaviour at the same time. For example, if puppy is sitting, then they cannot be jumping up (English Bull Terriers try, but to no avail!). In all of your future problem-solving, you'll be using MEBs a lot. It's like Kryptonite to unwanted behaviours!

Let me expand on this idea of MEBs. Don't want your dog to bark with excitement when you get home? Cool, teach them you'll only say hello when they're holding their favourite teddy (They can't bark *and* hold their teddy at the same time). Don't want your dog to pull on the lead to go over and play with their doggy pals? Okay, teach them that only when they give you eye contact will you say, 'Go play' and take them over for the meet-and-greet. They can't look at you *and* pull at the same time. Perfect MEB.

So, let me be clear: we're not going to punish puppy for jumping up, that's ridiculous. Punishment won't teach puppy *what* to do. It'll put you in a bad mood and it'll scare puppy. Not good.

## First Things First

Control and management (if you need a refresher, please see 'Control and Management is Your Best Friend', page 22). I'm the first to admit this, but sometimes we just don't have our 'Puppy Training' head on. Imagine the scene: you've had a hell of a day at work, you're on your last reserves of energy and patience and the doorbell goes. Your grandparents have popped around for five minutes.

You are midway through your 'no jumping up' training but puppy's not yet prepped to politely say 'Hi' to two equally excitable (and in this case, elderly) visitors. Especially two visitors who have previously been asked not to encourage and fuss puppy when he jumps up at them but merely replied, 'Oh, it's okay, we love puppies!'

Don't beat yourself up and don't set yourself (or puppy) up for failure. Do yourself a favour, pop puppy in the kitchen or garden with a nice stuffed Kong, answer the door and then go back to puppy in a few minutes. After the dust has settled, puppy can say hello to them on the lead (that's puppy on the lead, not the grandparents. Although...?) or through the child-gate to accommodate that initial, 'OH MY GOD, HUUUMANS!' outburst.

Here's the deal: your target, as ever, was to not let puppy practise and be *reinforced* for the unwanted behaviour. Mission accomplished.

## The Mutually Exclusive Behaviour

The trick here is to teach puppy *what* behaviour pays the dividends. What behaviour gives access to the desired goal?

I like 'Sit'.

Sit is a great Mutually Exclusive Behaviour to combat 'Jumping Up'.

Sit tends to be a behaviour that gets practised a lot, so let's use it to everyone's advantage to get puppy what they want. As always, if there is a behaviour we don't want, then we have to tell puppy what we *do* want instead.

Another approach with the same goal in mind would be to teach puppy that the doorbell = treats in their den. With enough repetition, puppy will hear the doorbell and rather than running to the front door, they'll run to their den. This exercise will also help with avoiding over-arousal when visitors arrive.

## WHAT TO DO WHEN A PUPPY JUMPS AT YOU

None of us are perfect. Good control and management is there to make it impossible for puppy to practise the unwanted behaviour, but you know what, sometimes we slip up. Sometimes we may forget and let the visitor into the kitchen before we've popped puppy on the lead or in the garden.

So, in comes Mrs Visitor.

You look at puppy, you look at Mrs Visitor, you strike a Macaulay Culkin 'Hands-to-Face' pose ...

Don't stress it.

If puppy runs and jumps up at Mrs Visitor, just ask her to stand still and *ignore* puppy. The important message here is that <u>WE DO NOT REINFORCE JUMPING UP</u>.

Wait.

Give it four to five seconds, if you've started your Automatic Sit training then we may be lucky enough that puppy has an 'Ah-ha!' moment and plants their butt. If so, awesome, immediately ask Mrs Visitor to crouch down and give little 'un a good fuss. If four to five seconds pass and puppy doesn't plant their butt, then ask puppy to sit and reinforce with a treat as above.

If puppy just can't sit due to the excitement of the situation, *c'est la vie*, tomorrow's another day. Take puppy outside for a moment, pop the lead on, then come back in and greet Mrs Visitor with the control you desire. Even if it means you come back in with a few treats and lure puppy into a sit before Mrs Visitor crouches down to say, 'Howdy Doody'.

Next time, improve your control and management; if needs be, put a big yellow 'C+M' Post-It note on your front door as a reminder!

## Avoid Any Telling Off, Shouting or Reprimanding

Picture the scene: imagine you walked into an appointment with someone and as you went to shake their hand they screamed 'No!' at you. Imagine you tried one more time and all they did was fold their arms and shout 'No!' louder. Not only would you be confused, inhibited and a little frightened, but you'll also be none the wiser as to what greeting you *should've* given.

Alternatively, imagine you enter the room and as you approach the person to shake their hand, they lift theirs and say, 'High Five'; you can then high five them (get you, hipster!). You'll get reinforced by having a nice greeting and then crack on with your appointment.

A high five might not have been the most natural way for you to say hello, but it did the trick, you still like the person you greeted and you'll know exactly what behaviour to do next time.

Win!

## PUPPIES WITH 'ANTS-IN-THEIR-PANTS'!

The sit, as explained above, is an awesome solution for the 'Serial Jumper' but some pups are just too darn fidgety to be able to plant their butt for more than a millisecond! If this is your little pup, then you need to teach this puppy an awesome 'Nose Target' (see page 209) – nose target is such a good trick to have up your sleeve that we will use it in other areas of your training and it will be referred to in its own chapter later in this book). Nose target is not only a great MEB to combat jumping up but it also helps the puppy (and owner) to be a little more proactive in getting the behaviours from each other that each so desire. So, for example: come in the door, as puppy heads towards you like a freight train, put out your hand out as you'll learn later in this book, give your cue 'Touch' and heavily reward with both a treat *and* the attention puppy craves. Everyone's a winner, baby!

# WHAT DOES THE DOORBELL PREDICT? 'DING DONG PUPPY'S GETTING HIGH ...'

Sometimes, puppies become so excited because they associate the doorbell with super-exciting visitors. This can make training very difficult and sometimes frustrating. Let's make it a more even playing field. Let's change the *association* of what the doorbell actually means to puppy.

The plan: relax in a comfy chair with puppy in the room with you. Have your training partner outside and, when planned, have them ring the doorbell, 'Ding-Dong'. As soon as the bell sounds, puppy may well get excited, but you're just going to get out of your chair and silently walk to the back of the house and drop a few tasty treats into puppy's bed. Pup will look at you, then the door, then you again and eventually head to their bed to get the treats.

Repeat several times per session. You youngsters can use your mobile phones to communicate with your Bell Ringing Helper to instruct the next Ding Dong (in the olden days, I used to have to send a fax, training sessions took years!).

With enough repetition, when the bell sounds, puppy will get up and go to the back of the house rather than the front door. This is conditioning at its finest and shows how to change the association and the emotional response to the sound of the doorbell.

Start stretching the duration between the cue (Ding Dong) and the treats at the back of the house – this is known as the 'Latency'. Just take your time getting out of your chair and slowly head towards the treat delivery area at the back of the house. This will help puppy replace the old doorbell reactivity with a fresh new impulse control and patience.

Now you can start adding distraction: 'Ding Dong' = pup goes to back of house = you go open / close the door = you go to back of house and treat puppy.

Evolve your training to the final picture which is Ding Dong = pup goes to back of house = you open the door and let Visitor in = call puppy to you = get a sit = reinforce puppy = High Five your new Visitor and tell them, 'Oh, pup's very good, yes, they've never jumped up at anyone!'

## CASE STUDY: Meet Big Dave!

Big Dave is a Bernese mountain dog. For those of you that don't know what a Bernese mountain dog looks like, imagine a cross between a Glam Rocker and an Oil Tanker. Huuuuge!

Bigger dog = bigger potential issue!

Big Dave lives with my friends Martin, Kaye and their two boys, and as a youngster he was perfect in every way. Almost. You guessed it, he was a serial 'Jumper Upperer'.

I think it was Oscar Wilde who said, 'To have a normal-size dog jump up at you can be a chore; to have a Bernese mountain dog jump up at you can be a real pain in the butt', so we had to address it swiftly.

The plan: turn Big Dave into a Sitting Boss.

The family were all on board and they practised Big Dave's sits in as many different environments as possible. Teaching inside and out, daytime and night. Even changing the way the cue of 'sit' was delivered by the family member: sometimes they were standing, sometimes seated. They even sometimes delivered the cue of 'sit' with their back to Big Dave to ensure that 'sit' meant 'sit', no matter what else was going on around them.

We reinforced the sit at every turn. When he wanted to play chase for a toy, we only threw it once his bum had hit the floor first. So, the sit was being reinforced with a retrieve. When he was out for a walk, he'd sit at a kerb before continuing to enjoy his walk. Reinforcement is in the eye of the beholder; there are so many opportunities to reinforce the behaviour you do want.

Another thread of our remedy was to make sure initial greetings to Big Dave were kept fairly short, to prevent his excitement building too much momentum. For starters, family members and visitors crouched down to Big Dave to say 'Hello'. Dave's mum Kaye was initially and understandably standing upright, he was a big fella and very excited on greeting her, so her reaction was to stay away from the action. However, that just put his target up high. I got her to crouch down to Big Dave's level, this was simple control and management. You can't jump up at someone if they are at your level, because you have nowhere to jump. Big Dave was getting the attention he wanted but without jumping up, so the behaviour was not being repeated and reinforced. During greetings, treats were also given on the floor for Big Dave to pick up rather than being placed in his mouth to reinforce the sit, that way Big Dave's overall focus was kept nice and low.

As a sensible control and management tool, we also introduced a puppy pen in part of the kitchen that Big Dave could be placed in, just in case any unbriefed visitors came into the kitchen (by 'unbriefed' I mean visitors that hadn't yet been told the 'Greeting Protocol', not naked visitors). The puppy pen was also used immediately after a particularly exciting greeting had been successfully executed with a sit to say 'Hi'. For example, visitor comes into kitchen – Big Dave sits – low greeting and chest rub delivered – handful of treats thrown into pen area for Big Dave to shift focus and enjoy without the risk of him reverting to 'Zebedee-Dog' and undoing his good work.

Here's another interesting observation of my time spent with this particular Bernese. Big Dave is a super-friendly dog and so strangers LOVED rubbing the top of his head as they passed by. Now, I appreciate it has been known for people to rub the top of a dog's head as they pass by but, I swear, Big Dave was like a magnet for wannabe Popes practising their blessings!

I think part of Big Dave's jumping up was to counter this predicted head rub when people approached him, his logic being if he could get his head high up above their hands, then problem solved, right?

Martin and Kaye were brilliant and spotted Big

Dave's slight discomfort with being patted on the noggin', so they learned to always intervene with a 'Oh, he loves having his chest rubbed', to avoid the strangers patting Big Dave's head for good luck.

Mutually exclusive behaviour, see? It's not just for dogs!

## CHAPTER 12

# REFLEX TO NAME (RTN)

## WHAT DOES IT LOOK LIKE?

Each time you say puppy's name, they can't resist checking in with you.

## WHY TEACH A REFLEX TO NAME?

Believe me, there's a lot of trouble puppy can get up to – or in to – when they're not checking in with you! A 'Reflex To Name' (RTN) response from puppy can act like 'power steering' to get puppy to focus on you, without you having to resort to pulling on the lead or other uncomfortable methods. Once trained, you can use your new powers of RTN to get puppy's attention anytime.

Have a read of the 'Reflex To Name' training method below, then grab yourself a cuppa, sit back and read the Case Study at the end to enjoy the torment I went through as I tried to teach the explosion that is Brian Blessed how sometimes, less is more!

## REFLEX TO NAME: THE PUPPY STEPS OF TRAINING

The method that follows is different from some of the other methods I've discussed because the delivery of the treat is *not* contingent initially on puppy's behaviour. We're not delivering a treat as a consequence to a behaviour, but merely pairing the sound of puppy's name with something good.

So, start in a nice quiet location with no distractions. Have plenty of small tasty treats in your treat pouch. If need be, have puppy attached by a lead to their harness.

For the purpose of this demonstration, my puppy will be called 'Colin' (I thank you).

Sit quietly with puppy.

After a few seconds of nothingness, say 'Colin' in a nice, cheery voice. Wait one second and then put a treat into Colin's mouth, *regardless of Colin's behaviour*. It's not important if he's not looking at you at this stage; what *is* important is that we are consistently 'charging the battery'. 'Colin' – wait one second – treat.

# Confidence

Build an optimistic and
confident super-pup!

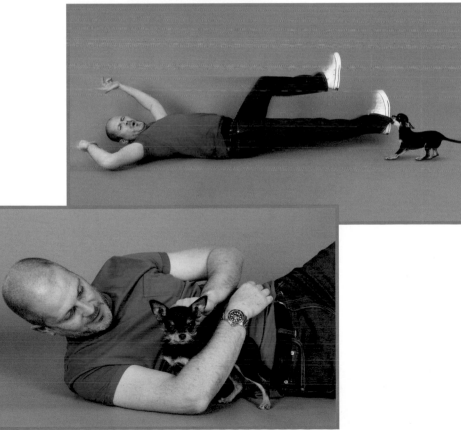

# Eye Contact

The one exercise that makes everything else easier.

Treats in the outstretched hand – say NOTHING. Only when pup looks to <u>you</u>, say 'Good' and reinforce!

# Loose Lead Walking

Eye contact stationary... then eye contact on the move.
Hey, presto – loose lead walking!

# Recall

The Matador Recall!

Through the legs.

Throw out the treat to the left.

Call back to you.

Then through the legs on the right.

Rinse and repeat, Olé!

# Nose Target

Nose to hand, say 'Good' and then treat.

Tip: To get started, channel your inner Mr Spock!

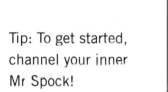

# The Puppy Den

Wrong.

Right.

Perfect!

# Teaching Abroad

I'm thankful every day for the opportunities I get to teach Dog Trainers and Behaviourists worldwide.

*Top*: Lecturing in Lithuania.

*Above left*: Teaching tracking dogs in South Africa.

*Above right*: Staff training in Bahrain.

*Right*: Visiting the amazing dogs of Peru, birthplace of the Rucksack Walk!

# My Life With Dogs

*Top left*: My Grandad's dog in Ireland, Buff. His previous dog was also called Buff. His next dog? Buff.

*Top right*: I loved that damn 'dog'!

*Middle right*: My heart and soul. Me and Alfacakes would play like this for hours. I would give anything for another five minutes.

*Below right*: From Freaky Dog Boy to TV Dog Trainer. Appearing on ITV with Lorraine Kelly and Angela Griffin.

That's the deal.

100%. Every time.

After another few seconds ... 'Colin' – wait one second – deliver treat.

Wait five seconds, repeat. 'Colin' – wait one second – deliver treat.

Wait three seconds, repeat...

One second, repeat...

Ten seconds, repeat...

Do 25 repetitions.

In-between repetitions say nothing. The learning will be cleaner if we can cut out all peripheral distractions such as other words and movements.

Do three to four sessions a day.

Ensure you are delivering the treat one second *after* 'Colin' and ensure you are not looking for, or even expecting, any behaviour as a response at this time. Then, when that has been solidly practised, change location, then also vary the time of day and, if other humans live with Colin, vary the trainer.

Also, don't always have the treats on you. We don't want to teach puppy that it's only worthwhile them tuning in to you if you're wearing your treat pouch, as that can be very limiting in real-life situations. Therefore, in some of your training sessions, have the treats away from you, perhaps in a bowl on a shelf or on the other side of the room. Everything else remains the same, so say 'Colin' then in this case run over to the shelf and deliver the treat. Then go back to the original starting position away from the treats and repeat...

Once you have a nice reliable RTN (even if it's not puppy's actual name you're using), you can start to 'take it on the road'. Introduce it into your loose lead walking routines if you'd like puppy to check in with you more frequently, or even use it as a much more constructive and positive alternative to the big growly 'LEAVE IT!' you may have been tempted to use once or twice in the past.

Although we always want to be 'training' and not 'testing', over time you won't be able to ignore the beautiful 'head snap' that puppy does when you say their name. There's the magic!

You now have added a conditioned 'Reflex To Name' to your puppy training toolbox. Have the rest of the day off!

## A WORD OF CAUTION

Remember when someone kept calling you at school, it got quite tiresome and you eventually said, 'That's my name, don't wear it out!'

Well, Colin feels the same!

For this exercise to be as potent as possible, it's important that we don't use puppy's name indiscriminately. Colin at this stage must always predict that something super-cool is following. If you live in a busy household full of people saying, 'Colin-this' and 'Colin-that', then I recommend you use a new, unique word for your RTN training. So, rather than using puppy's name, use a one or two syllable phrase that you will use for what puppy should feel is *always* a special occasion. As a one-off, sale-of-the-century-deal-and-for-today-only, I'm giving these words away for free!

– *Pup-Pup!*

– *Baby!*

– *Yip!*

Choose one and use it wisely. It's yours. Free!

---

### 🔍 CASE STUDY: My Brian Blessed Story

I was lucky enough to be the winning trainer on the BBC TV programme *The Underdog Show*, which took 10 of the UK's leading dog trainers, and paired them with 10 celebrities to train 10 rescue dogs on a weekly 'live' TV show hosted by Julian Clary. Due to our success on series one (why, thank you!), I was asked to return on series two as Head Judge.

Now, one of the celebrities on series two was the legend that is Brian Blessed who was training a

---

pointer mix called Dougal. If you don't know who Brian Blessed is, he's the larger than life BOOMING actor who played such wallflowers as Prince Vultan in *Flash Gordon*, Long John Silver in *Treasure Island* and, my favourite, Grampy Rabbit in *Peppa Pig*. If you still don't know who Brian Blessed is, imagine being trapped inside a kaleidoscope made out of foghorns and volume.

During a quiet time in filming, Brian mentioned to me that he was struggling to get Dougal to focus on him when in front of the cameras. He wanted Dougal to focus on him in the same way that I had trained Chump to focus on Selina Scott in series one.

Now, remember, how you deliver your name and cues is *very* important. If you just rattle off lots of words and the key word is hidden somewhere in that rambling sentence, then how on earth is a puppy supposed to know what to do? It's like me listening to a rap song full of hundreds of words but then being expected to easily pick out and act upon one word from that mass of lyrics. When you do that with a puppy, they think, *I've got to respond to everything here or ignore everything here*. They simply can't think, *Okay, ignore that, ignore that, ignore that, ah! Act on that, then ignore that...*

So, when you give a cue it's much better that it's one syllable, succinct, unique and consistent.

So, there I am, with the legend that is Brian Blessed and I'm trying to teach him the initial stages of 'Reflex To Name', as per above.

Me:  Okay, Brian, I just want you to say, 'Dougal' once, then treat.

The legend that is Brian Blessed:  NOW DOUGAL, OH DOUGAL, YES, THAT'S IT, WHATTA BOY, OH, DOUGAL NOW THEN...

Me:  Like that, Brian, yes. But this time, just say *one* word, 'Dougal', nothing else. Then treat.

The legend that is Brian Blessed:  Right you are, Steve ... AHHHH, DOUGAL MY BOY, WHATTA FELLA, WHATTA FELLA, EH, THAT'S MY BOY, NOW, YOU LOOK HERE, DOUGIE OLD BOY...

Me:  Nearly there, Brian. If you can, and I *know* you can, just say the one word 'Dougal' and nothing else. That way we're going to condition a perfect Reflex To Name.

The legend that is Brian Blessed:   OH, WAS I NOT, DEAR BOY? CRIKEY. RIGHTO, HERE WE GO ... NOW, DOUGAL, OH, YOU ARE A BEAUUUUTIFUL CREATURE, YES, YOU ARE, HERE WE GO, BOY, YES, WE DO, OH YEEEEES ... WE DO...

Me:   Spot on, Brian. Good luck with tonight's show!

# CHAPTER 13

# EYE CONTACT

'The keys to the kingdom come
via Eye Contact.'

## WHY TEACH EYE CONTACT?

Without doubt, this is the one exercise that makes all other exercises easier. If I had to name one exercise as my number one, this is it! It is the foundation of everything else in this book. Simply put, if puppy's not looking at you, there's a pretty good chance that they're not listening to you either! Done correctly, strong and reliable 'Eye Contact' can be the spine of everything else.

I want puppy to always be thinking:

🐾 If there's something in it for me, look up to the monkey.

*e.g. engage with my owner for play time.*

🐾 If I want to gain access to something, look up to the monkey.
*e.g. release off lead to play with other dogs.*

🐾 If I feel nervous or scared, look up to the monkey.
*e.g. toddler approaching on a scooter.*

Unusually, I don't add a verbal cue for eye contact. As above, I want puppy to offer eye contact to make the good stuff happen, as opposed to me having to ask for it. Chances are, if I'm in a situation and I feel the need to get puppy to look at me, the horse has already bolted. Maybe figuratively, maybe literally!

I love the idea that puppy is always thinking, *How can I train this monkey to...*

🐾 *Cross the road with me?*

🐾 *Give me a cue?*

🐾 *Open the back door?*

🐾 *Throw the ball?*

🐾 *Keep walking along the pavement with me on the lead?*

Answer: look up at the monkey!

We've previously talked about 'cues' for behaviour in terms of words, but actually cues come in several forms, so let me explain that and give you some examples. As dog trainers (as that is what you now are, like it or not!), we tend to think of cues being our vocal commands, our 'Sit' and our 'Come!' and so on. But cues can come from the surrounding environment *as well as* from our mouths. For example:

🐾 Opening the den door may be puppy's cue to run in.

🐾 Opening the treat packet may be puppy's cue to sit pretty!

🐾 Hearing the doorbell may be puppy's cue to go nuts or go find you. The decision is yours, reinforce the behaviour you want more of in the future!

So, I like puppy to make the first move in offering me eye contact, if at all possible. If I <u>do</u> need to ask puppy to look to me, perhaps we're at the vets and I've spotted a little old lady wandering towards us with an occupied cat carrier before puppy has seen them. Well, I can then ask for a 'Reflex To Name' (see page *167*) or do a little 'Recall' (page *197*).

Eye contact is also an awesome 'Mutually Exclusive Behaviour' (see page *155*) to counter many 'problem' behaviours (they tend to be more of a problem for the owner than they are for the puppy!). For example:

🐾 Puppy can't pull on the lead during a walk if they're glancing up to you.

🐾 Puppy can't be barking at other dogs to 'go play' if they're glancing up to you.

🐾 Puppy can't be bouncing and jumping up at the child in the park you're chatting to if they're glancing up to you.

You get the picture. Convinced? Cool, let's crack on with the training:

## EYE CONTACT: THE PUPPY STEPS OF TRAINING

1. Sit on the floor with puppy and have a handful of treats in your closed fist. Hold your treat-laden fist out in front of you.

2. Say *nothing*. (This is the hardest part of the exercise, particularly for men!) Let puppy lick your hand, paw your hand, etc. They will try a host of various behaviours to get at the treats. Our skill here is in waiting until we get the behaviour we want.

3. Keep your eyes fixed on puppy's face, then the *second* they glance up at you say 'Good!', and give them a treat from the hand. As ever, don't be too greedy here; a glance towards your upper body at this stage is enough to make you say 'Good' and deliver the treat. As your repetitions progress, we can raise the criteria and 'shape' the behaviour from a 'torso glance' to 'Eye Contact'. Anyway, let's continue...

4. Let puppy enjoy and finish each treat. Then bring your treat-laden hand around to the front again and do another repetition.

We need three vital ingredients for this exercise, and in fact for all exercises, to be as effective as possible:

1. **Motivation:** is puppy super-motivated for the treats? If not, get better treats or train initially in a less distracting location or at a different time of day. Remember, puppies don't *lose* focus, they only *change* focus.

2. **Patience:** relax, it's not a race. As long as you can see that puppy is motivated for the food, then, through trial and error, puppy will figure out what behaviour pays dividends. (My dad

used to say, 'Patience is a virtue, have it if you can, it's seldom in a puppy, and never in a man!')

3. **Timing**: for puppy to realise *exactly* what behaviour paid the dividends, make sure you have the timing of a Ninja by saying 'Good!' the *second* puppy's eyes look to yours, *then* deliver the treat.

The fact that you're saying 'Good' to 'mark' the behaviour means that you don't have to be in a rush to deliver the food. For perfect conditioning, ensure you say 'Good' *then* start the process of moving your hand to feed. *Separate the two actions.* If you don't 'mark' the behaviour with a 'Good', then puppy will still enjoy the food, but they won't know why they got it, which means they won't know what behaviour to repeat next time.

As with all exercises, *repeat, repeat, repeat.*

Do the above in a variety of locations to *proof* the behaviour (see page 88) and remember to initially keep your sessions short and sweet. If motivation is good, you should get a good 10 to 15 'Eye Contacts' to reinforce in a five to ten-minute session. You're much better to do several short sessions in various locations throughout the day, than a marathon session that will see a tapering off of motivation, reinforcement and, therefore, progress.

## ADDING DURATION

For the above points 1-4, we've focused on initially getting and then immediately reinforcing the behaviour of eye contact. For real-life scenarios when you'll want that eye contact for longer (as the scary dog walks by, for example) and to build your 'connection stamina', let's start adding a bit of duration to your training:

1. Complete the above steps until your pup's a 'looking machine'!

2. When pup gives you eye contact, wait one second before saying 'Good' and reinforcing. Repeat, repeat, repeat.

3. When pup gives you eye contact, wait two seconds before saying 'Good' and reinforcing. Repeat, repeat, repeat.

4. Over time, increase the eye contact duration within each session; however, throw a cheeky little one-or two-second short one every now and then to keep puppy engaged and never quite knowing when the 'Good' will come. Think payouts on a 'fruit machine', rather than a vending machine!

# FUNK IT UP!

So, as soon as you sit down with pup and place your loaded fist out in front of you, are you getting immediate eye contact? Yes? Great, then let's get funky with it!

Keep the common denominator of *pup looks to you = 'Good' = treat*, but change the picture every now and then to ensure that no matter what else is going on around you, you can rely on a rock-solid eye contact behaviour from puppy.

Do the exercise from a chair; do it standing up; or, if you're feeling cheeky, do it lying down. Do it by the school gates, near the ice-cream van or at the park.

Contrary to popular belief, practice *does not* make perfect. *Perfect* practice makes perfect, so make sure you set the correct criteria and work through all of the many distractions you can think of to earn yourself the perfect puppy eye contact.

## CASE STUDY: Lorraine and Angus

I've had the pleasure to guest on ITV's *Lorraine* show a couple of times with Lorraine Kelly and her cracking little Border terrier pup, Angus. Lorraine was having the usual puppy problems like play-biting, toilet training, recall, introducing Angus to other dogs, etc. However, what was brilliant about her approach was that she was taking Angus into the studio pretty much from the word go. When we talk about training with distractions, I'm not sure there's a much more distracting environment than a live TV studio! Because Angus is lucky enough to go to work with Lorraine each day, it was essential we taught him eye contract straight-away so he and Lorraine were always on the same 'frequency', regardless of what was going on around them. They have a great relationship because Angus knows that checking in with 'Mum' is the conduit to all good things including training, affection, fun and safety. That's all thanks to eye contact and Lorraine's hard work.

## CHAPTER 14

# LOOSE LEAD WALKING

## WHAT IS LOOSE LEAD WALKING AND WHY DO YOU NEED TO TEACH IT?

Puppy is walking alongside you in a relaxed and happy manner. You're holding the lead which is attached to puppy's harness and as the pair of you walk with each other, the lead is 'smiling'. It's so important for puppy's quality of life that they regularly go for walks with you to enjoy exploring and interacting with the 'outside' world. Walking with your puppy has the potential to be one of the most enjoyable activities of your lives together. It also has the potential to be one of the most miserable experiences you could ever imagine if you don't teach correct 'Loose Lead Walking'! Unnecessary tension on the lead can cause physical (and mental!) strains on both of you.

## WHY DO DOGS PULL ON THE LEAD?

Dominance? Nope!

They want to be Pack Leader? Nope!

They generally walk faster than humans? Yep!

Our job is to teach them that walking 'with' us is the behaviour that pays the best dividends. The quickest way to get to the good stuff – the next great smell, the park, the other dog – is to walk together on a slack lead.

## LOOSE LEAD WALKING: THE PUPPY STEPS OF TRAINING

As per the previous chapter, if puppy is checking in with you when you're *stationary*, you've got 'Eye Contact'. If puppy's checking in with you *on the move*, you've got 'Loose Lead Walking'! You've already built the foundation of your loose lead walking by investing in eye contact, so let's just move it up a notch and blend eye contact into loose lead walking. We're working on the theory that if puppy is looking at you on the move, they can't pull on the lead at the same time.

1.  Start off-lead. Be standing, have your treat-laden

fist in front of you. Slowly walk backwards in tiny steps so pup follows you; once they look at you on the move say 'Good!' and reinforce.

2. Repeat your tiny backward steps and reinforce each time puppy looks at you on the move.

3. Change your direction: rather than walking backwards, take tiny steps to the side, left to right, or walk in a slow arch. As ever, when puppy looks at you on the move say 'Good' and reinforce. This is good stuff!

4. As above, but now have the light lead attached to puppy's harness as an added distraction. 'Mark' and reinforce any eye contact on the move. Be careful not to tread on the lead, move slowly with tiny steps at this stage.

5. As above, but hold the lead.

6. As above, but change location.

7. As above, but start walking more in a forward, 'normal' motion with standard stride lengths.

8. Use as many locations as possible to 'proof' the behaviour.

Hey Presto, your pup's a 'Loose Lead Walker'! You'll both get to enjoy your walks in comfort. Puppy's delicate body will not be damaged by pulling on a tight lead and you'll get to keep both of your collar bones. Win!

As you've already uploaded the eye contact 'software' into puppy, it's an awesome behaviour to then upgrade into loose lead walking; however, the beauty of dog training is as long as you know your ingredients, you can come up with as many different recipes as you fancy. Let's have a look at some other loose lead walking techniques below...

## DRUNK DOG WALKING

I developed 'Drunk Dog Walking' during my many years of teaching puppy group classes as a great way to get quick success. I guess some day I should add one of those funky little ™ or © signs but you know what, *mi casa es su casa*.

Start with puppy on a nice long lead, approximately 1.5 metres in length, attached to their comfortable harness. Have your two hands together by your belt buckle area. If you're the type to instinctively grab further down the lead, therefore making the lead unnecessarily tight, then have your two hands together and pop your two thumbs down the top of your trousers. There, that's *your* 'Mutually Exclusive Behaviour' sorted! Have your treat pouch clipped onto your waist and make sure it's loaded with plenty of small but amazing treats. Before you set off, reinforce a few repetitions of the eye contact exercise so puppy knows it's time to tune in.

1. You're going to very slowly walk no more than five steps in any one direction in a style that is as 'un-dog-trainer-like-fashion' as possible. No fast straight lines, no 90 degree turns (what is it with dog trainers and 90 degree turns? I've never seen anyone walk that way down the park!). Take nice small steps; some out to the front, now in a crescent, now backwards. Super-slow, super-small and constantly changing direction. You know, the kind of hesitant steps you take at 3am on a Saturday morning when you're trying to aim your key into your front door? Hence the name: 'Drunk Dog Walking'.

2. Here's the deal: if, as you move, the lead is slack, say 'Good' and give puppy a treat. Ideally, give the treat to your puppy 'on the move'. It's a great opportunity for puppy to learn that *good stuff sometimes comes from the monkey when we're walking*, as well as when you're stationary. If we only ever treat the puppy when we're standing still, puppy will soon zone out when we're on the move.

# REINFORCEMENT PLACEMENT

Puppies, like us, hang out where the good stuff is. If, in the future, we want puppy to walk on our left-hand side, then that's where the treats should be delivered to. If we want puppy to be walking on our right-hand side, that's cool, just make sure that is where the reinforcement delivery occurs. (N.B. there's this time-honoured (nonsense) rule in many dog training clubs that dogs should walk on the owner's left-hand side. This is just one of those indoctrinated rules that rarely gets questioned. Have you ever asked why? The original reason was that back in the day when dog training was only targeted towards military handlers, all dogs were trained to 'Heel' on the left-hand side so that the handler could still have easy access to reach and fire their gun. Today, in puppy classes, I hardly ever ask owners to shoot someone, so it's now a moot point. Do what's most comfortable for you.)

After several short sessions, it's time to raise the bar. Set off as before, and for the first few repetitions of slack lead say 'Good' and treat. The next time you're slowly moving and the lead is slack, don't automatically say 'Good' or treat ... *wait*.

What we're looking for here is for puppy to say to themselves, *I'm walking here next to my buddy and I don't feel any tight lead tension on my harness so I'm due a treat. Where's my treat?*

The *second* they glance up to you in anticipation as if to say, 'Oi! Where's my treat?!' *then* you say 'Good!' and reinforce.

Now we have a new criteria and we're actually giving the treat as a consequence to the behaviour of puppy looking up and 'checking in' with you on the move. Eye contact on the move – the loose lead walking stuff of dreams!

Don't be in too much of a hurry here: despite what other books and trainers will tell you, loose lead walking is bloomin' hard! Take it steady and, as always, consolidate your training in as many different locations as possible to get a nice strong foundation.

Initially keep sessions short: five to ten minutes per session is great to start off with. Let puppy know it's 'Training Time', which should always translate as 'Fun Time' or 'The Window Of Awesome Opportunity Has Just Opened Time!' or TWOFOHJOT* for short. (*Although this may also be a wardrobe from IKEA.)

I like to let puppy know it's 'Training Time' by having a little play as I say, 'Wanna do a bit of training, buddy?' I'll then do a few repetitions of eye contact to get us in the zone. Sounds silly, I know, but it's a nice way for us both to focus on each other. Imagine having dancing lessons but never knowing when they're taking place; you'd be all over the place!

## ADDING OUR THREE DS

Once you're walking a few steps together and puppy is looking up to you every now and then, we can begin to manipulate our Three Ds. You're familiar with the concept of the Three Ds now, but here it is in relation to loose lead walking:

**Distance**: rather than rewarding as soon as the lead is slack on the move, see if you can go two or three steps with the lead still 'smiling' before you say 'Good' and reinforce. Then four to five steps, then over five steps...

**Duration**: rather than rewarding as soon as the lead is slack on the move, or focusing on the number of steps before reinforcing, try changing your pace, sometimes two to three quick little steps, sometimes two to three slo-mo little steps. The criteria you're setting here is the *duration* of slack lead. Reinforce after two to three seconds of slack lead on the move, then four to five, then over five seconds.

**Distraction**: as above, but by practising in various locations you will naturally be training in environments of differing distractions. However, always aim for success. If a particular environment is too distracting for puppy, then it's simply too distracting for them. Relocate from that area or just relax, don't worry about your loose lead walking for now and just sit with puppy to let them watch, learn and absorb the environment around them. If they need to check it out, they need to check it out. Don't get into a conflict with them by insisting on being a Trainy-Trainer-Head.

Tomorrow's another day.

Your relationship comes first.

## THE ANTI-DOG TRAINER METHOD OF LOOSE LEAD WALKING

Here's one to upset all the pros!

On the face of it, the method I've developed below may seem a little topsy-turvy and I guess it is, but there's a method in the madness, so let me explain...

Our target is for puppy not to pull on the lead.

Definition of pulling on the lead = walking several steps with the lead tight between puppy and handler.

What if we could invent a self-correcting puppy? We'll be rich, rich, I tell ya!

### Self-Correcting: The Puppy Steps of Training

1. Do a few repetitions of your eye contact exercise, with you standing nice and still. This will get

puppy in the zone and also, importantly, remind them that 'Good!' predicts a treat from you.

2. Hold the lead full length, with two hands together by your belt buckle area. Slowly start walking, small steps, in a straight line.

3. *As soon* as the lead goes tight, say 'Good' and give puppy a treat. Head. Explodes.

Don't worry. You're *not* reinforcing pulling on the lead here. What you are doing is building your self-correcting puppy. Trust me on this one, I do it for a living!

Remember, the definition of pulling on the lead is walking *several* steps with the lead tight between puppy and handler. By you giving puppy a treat the split-second the lead goes tight, the predictor for the treat becomes 'tight lead'.

Now we have a two-stage process:

1. Tight lead = 'Good' = treat from handler

2. Tight lead = look back to handler in anticipation of treat = 'Good' = treat

Do a few repetitions of (1) to build the relationship between tight lead and checking in with you. Once you see evidence that puppy is looking back to you when the lead is tight before you've even said 'Good', then you can move on to stage (2). As soon as puppy knows what the predictor of the treat is, and as long as they're motivated for the food, there's no way they'll continue to pull on the lead.

This method gives us an opportunity to crack on and progress with our training nice and quickly. Once we've reinforced puppy 'self-correcting' and looking back to us, we can then carry on from a more logical standpoint, which is: reinforce puppy intermittently as they walk with you on a slack lead. Constantly adjusting distance, distraction and duration as appropriate.

## FUNK IT UP!

Don't be afraid to throw other cheeky little cues that you've already taught puppy into your loose lead walking sessions. For example, a few steps then a 'Sit' or some downright funky cues that you'll learn later in this book such as 'Nose Target' and 'To the Fridge!'

## 🔍 CASE STUDY: The Dog Said Nothing

True story! One of my all-time favourite sightings down the park was when I was out doing a one-to-one loose lead training session with an owner and dog in Richmond Park. (By the way, Richmond Park is home of the YouTube 'Fenton' sensation. If you think *your* pup has a bad recall, treat yourself to 0.47 seconds of pure YouTube madness!)

Anyhoo, the owner and dog I was training were doing fantastically well and walking along the path with a lovely loose 'smiling' lead to consolidate all they had learned. Coming along the path in the other direction was a guy with a German shepherd on the lead and to say the dog was pulling would be a massive understatement. The guy looked both exhausted and completely exasperated. In a last-ditch effort to stop his dog pulling, he stopped, walked around to face the dog and with a pointed finger said, 'Look! We spoke about this before we left home!'

The dog said nothing.

I gave the man my card.

## CHAPTER 15

# RECALL

### WHAT DOES A RECALL LOOK LIKE?

As soon as you call 'Come!' puppy comes thundering towards you with the speed of a puma!

### WHY TEACH A RECALL?

If you ever plan to have puppy off-lead outside, it's essential that you have an *epic* 'Recall' for safety and to ensure each outing is as pleasurable as possible for both of you. Potentially, a brilliant recall might actually save your puppy's life if they are running off towards a road or other dangerous situation. It's *that* important.

# RECALL: THE PUPPY STEPS OF TRAINING

We're actually spoilt for choice on how to teach a 'Recall', so I've added a few bonus tracks to the album for you. Below are several methods and techniques to train puppy to be a 'Total Recaller'! Don't just choose one method; do them all in different sessions and in different locations to keep your training interesting and fun.

A few notes before we start: for all recalls, we want to be reinforcing puppy *running* to you, not just a slow walk or trot. We'll ultimately get what we reinforce and if a slow, unmotivated meander is considered 'good enough' in your controlled training sessions, then the recall will easily be knocked off track when we 'go live' down the park with the added distractions of dogs, birds and fox poo!

We want your cue of 'Come!' to always be super-friendly as it needs to predict that great things are coming from you for puppy. NEVER call puppy in an angry voice, no matter how tempting! An angry voice or body language *does not* predict great things are coming from you for puppy, therefore you'll 'poison' your cue, leading to a hesitant recall in the future.

We also always want your recall cue to be super-potent. We do not want puppy to get in the habit of ignoring

your cue as that will dilute its potency in the future and the standards will deteriorate. If you're not prepared to bet £100 that puppy will come to you on the first call of 'Come!' then don't call them. Go over and get puppy yourself. The exercise will be good for you!

And finally, pay well. Like I said, a good recall could be a lifesaver. It's a great investment, so be generous with the reinforcement.

## THE RESTRAINED RECALL

For this exercise, we need two people (you and one other, let's call him 'Woodhouse')

1. Have Woodhouse crouch down and gently hold puppy by their harness while you show them the treats in your hand.

2. Run away, as Woodhouse continues to hold puppy's harness. Once you're 10 metres or so away, have Woodhouse release puppy to sprint towards you. As soon as puppy is running towards you, keep jogging and shout 'COME!' in a loud and happy voice. What we're doing above is pairing the behaviour of 'running to you' with the cue 'Come!' We want to train and to practise for what we'll ultimately need when

we're down the park. You'll be calling puppy in a loud voice when they're a distance away from you, so start conditioning as you mean to go on to make sure your cue remains consistent.

3. As soon as puppy catches up to you, crouch down, give them a big fuss and reward them with the treats you're holding.

4. Repeat as above several times. Then repeat again but start saying 'Come!' *just before* Woodhouse releases puppy to run to you. Now we've got everything in the correct order: 'Come!' = puppy running to you = reinforcement = (a happy puppy + a happy you) = a happy me!

5. Extra tip: to maintain puppy's speed as they catch up to you, try throwing the treats in the direction puppy is running just before they get to you.

## FUNK IT UP!

Once you're flying through stages 1–4 as above, let's funk it up a little by turning you into a 'Recalling Matador'!

1. As puppy catches up to you, face puppy and throw the treat between your legs, encouraging

puppy to then also go between your legs to get the treat. This will increase the speed of recall because they accelerate right up to and through your legs, rather than hitting the brakes five metres away.

2. Turn and face puppy, as they finish their treat as above and then look up to you, say 'Come!' and throw another treat between your legs for puppy to chase after.

3. As puppy eats, jog away IN THE OPPOSITE DIRECTION to increase the distance between you, THEN face puppy again to make the recall game even more fun by turning it into an exciting game of 'catch up' or 'chase'.

4. Each time puppy sprints between your legs to get their reward, add more and more distance to the next repetition.

5. N.B. you do not need to say, 'Olé'!

## RECALL CIRCUITS

This is a lovely recall exercise to do if you're restricted to a small area or if you don't have your own personal 'Woodhouse' to call upon! It's also a nice exercise to transfer to the park, as the small space required means you'll be less likely to bump into potential distractions coming up over the horizon.

1. Use three markers (such as flower pots) or just your imagination to lay out a triangle on the ground, with three sides approximately 10 strides in length. Stand at point one with puppy. Say 'Come!', quickly place three or four treats on the ground by your feet and as puppy begins to eat, you sneak away to point two. Even though puppy is stood next to you, still shout 'Come!' prior to placing the treats on the ground. It's a free opportunity to show puppy what the sound of 'Come!' actually predicts (good stuff!).

2. You're now stood by point two, facing puppy as they eat the treats from the ground back at point one. As soon as puppy finishes the treats and looks up, you shout 'Come!' and place a further three or four treats by your feet.

3. As soon as puppy gets to you at point two to eat their treats, you run away to point three.

4. As soon as puppy looks up from finishing their treats at point two, shout, 'Come!' from position three and place three or four treats at your feet for puppy to run to.

5. Repeat ... forever!

Don't just use one piece of food per drop (you miser!). The reason I want you to use three or four pieces is the extra time required for puppy to pick up the food will give you the time necessary to make good your getaway to the next point of the triangle. Over time this will also help you add distance to your recalls.

## FULCRUM RECALLS

Don't fancy all the energy-sapping exercise required in the previous two recall exercises? Should've got a goldfish then, eh?!

Okay, for 'Fulcrum Recall' training you really don't have to break out of a slow walk and it's a really nice exercise to blend into your normal walks. It's called the fulcrum because you are the 'centre' of all the puppy's movements.

1. Let puppy see you throw a treat out to your left-hand side.

2. As puppy eats the treat and then looks up, say, 'Come!' and as puppy runs to you, throw a treat out to your right-hand side.

3. You can continue a slow and steady walk, wait

until puppy looks up and then say 'Come!' and throw a treat back out to your left-hand side.

This is a nice, informal exercise that you can blend into your walks at random intervals. You're reinforcing the recalls but also puppy is learning that it's worth their while to keep an eye on you when out and about in anticipation of the recall game commencing again!

## 'CAPTURING' THE RECALL

If puppy just happens to offer a behaviour you love, like coming to you on a walk, even if you haven't cued it, then 'capture' the behaviour by reinforcing it with a great treat. If the 'captured' behaviour is reinforced, then that behaviour becomes more likely to occur again in the future. You'll be surrounded by opportunities to capture and reinforce great behaviours offered by puppy, so don't miss your chance to fill pup's 'list of things to do' with the behaviours you love! *What gets treated gets repeated!*

To constantly improve puppy's recall, make sure you do the above exercises in a constant variety of locations to really 'proof' the behaviour and make it as reliable as possible. No matter what others may say (brag), *no* dog has a completely 100% perfectly reliable recall, so appreciate that it is, and always will be, a work in progress.

Enjoy the journey.

# THE EMERGENCY RECALL

But what if puppy gets loose by accident before I've taught a recall? What if I discover the recall I thought I taught isn't as reliable as I thought I'd taught it! What if puppy is off-lead and the little tinker won't come back?

Okay, so if this happens, then this isn't a training opportunity, it's an *emergency*. If you're built for speed (e.g. you're Usain Bolt), and your puppy isn't (e.g. they're a bulldog!), then run and grab your puppy before they get into trouble. However, if your puppy is playing 'stay away' and you know you're not going to catch them, then try one of the below:

- Lay on the floor and kick your legs up in the air as you make weird noises. (I bet you wish you taught a better recall now!) The whole weirdness of the situation will often serve to draw the curious puppy back to you.

- Run in the opposite direction away from puppy. This may hopefully encourage puppy to chase you in fear of being abandoned.

- Pull out puppy's favourite toy and start whooping and playing with it yourself. If you look like you're having the time of your life, hopefully puppy will want a piece of the action, too.

As I say, none of the above three methods are training tools, they're merely emergency options if you haven't yet taught a bullet-proof recall.

The most important point about recall is perhaps this simple fact: be careful when out with puppy, don't let them off-lead if it's not safe to do so, they're just too precious.

> ## 🔍 CASE STUDY: A Cautionary Tale!
>
> Not only is having a poor recall potentially dangerous, but it can also cost you a fair few quid! I was lucky enough to be recruited to help train TV presenter Graham Norton's dog, Bailey, who was a real 'life-loving' labradoodle, when he was around two years old. The first time I met Graham, he told me that, like all good, responsible dog owners, before he headed out for a dog walk he would grab the lead, some spare poo bags and plenty of treats. However, due to Bailey's habit of ignoring his recall cue in favour of raiding the conveniently spread picnics around Hyde Park, Graham also had to make sure that along with packing the treats and poo bags before a walk, he also had to grab a fresh supply of tenners from the ATM as he was constantly running in Bailey's wake handing out

compensatory £10 notes to those who now had paw prints all over their quiche lorraine!

We decided to take it back a few steps, so we taught Bailey the value of 'Come' in a much less distracting environment. Over the weeks, we worked on recall circuits and, at any given opportunity, we reinforced Bailey every time he voluntarily checked in with Graham when out on walks. Importantly, we didn't have Bailey off-lead in any areas in which we weren't confident that he could immediately, and successfully, respond to our recall.

Over time, as Bailey's recall became more and more robust in an ever-expanding number of distracting environments, Graham was eventually able to continue his dog walking in Hyde Park without having to wrestle the odd Scotch egg from Bailey's mush.

CHAPTER 16

# NOSE TARGET

## WHAT DOES A NOSE TARGET LOOK LIKE?

You hold out your hand, say 'Touch' and puppy touches their nose against your hand!

## WHY TEACH NOSE TARGET?

A good nose target has lots of potentially great benefits that aren't offered by other exercises. It can:

- Build a positive association with human hands.
- Encourage 'four feet on the floor' when greeting people.

- Maintain a still position during handling exercises, such as grooming or health treatments.

- Turn puppy's attention to you if you're in the presence of someone that isn't comfortable around dogs.

## NOSE TARGET: THE PUPPY STEPS OF TRAINING

1. Place a treat between the third and fourth finger of your right hand (think Mr Spock!).

2. Make sure puppy's attention is on you and place your right hand behind your back.

3. From behind your back, present your right hand in front of you 30 centimetres from puppy's nose. The novelty of your freshly presented hand coupled with the lure of the treat between your fingers will entice puppy to move their nose towards your hand.

4. *As soon as* puppy's nose touches your hand, say 'Good!', then put your right hand back behind your back and reinforce with a treat *from your other hand*. The reason you do not reinforce with the treat in your 'target' hand is that

we don't want puppy to learn it's only worth touching the hand if there's a treat in it. The reason you 'produce' and 'remove' your right hand prior to, and after, the nose touch is to keep the presentation of the right hand unique, and therefore part of the cue. Pups are curious creatures so they're more likely to want to 'check out' the hand if it's just appeared.

5. After several successful repetitions, try a few without the lure (treat) between your right-hand fingers.

6. Once the behaviour is nice and fluent, starting adding the cue 'Touch' as you present your hand (get the behaviour, say 'Good' and reinforce with a treat as before). The reason we want to put this behaviour on a vocal cue is because sometimes we will want to ask for the behaviour when puppy isn't necessarily looking at us.

## ADDING DURATION

A quick 'Touch' cue followed by the desired behaviour will give us the attention we need to steer puppy away from the dreaded ice cream or perhaps to get a mutually exclusive behaviour instead of jumping up at people. However, if we can get a nose touch with a longer duration, then we can use the behaviour for handling and grooming sessions, too. To do this:

1. Continue as page 210 with the Puppy Steps of Training.

2. Progress to give your cue – 'Touch' – then when puppy puts their nose to your hand, rather than saying 'Good' as soon as contact is made, wait one second, *then* – and only if the nose is still touching – say 'Good' and reinforce with a treat. Over time, increase the duration of the touch with each session.

3. As with all exercises, to raise the criteria, manipulate the Three Ds.

## FUNK IT UP!

Okay, so now we're getting plenty of nose touches from puppy when we're asking for them. Let's change the context with some of the examples below to really *proof* the behaviour and to make it a little funkier for you both!

🐾 Get a 'Touch' then throw the treat a few metres away from you for puppy to chase and eat. As soon as puppy looks back up after having eaten the treat, say 'Touch', offer your hand and when puppy's nose touches your hand, then mark and *reinforce* as before by throwing another treat. This method puts more animation into the exercise and is a great foundation for your recall training. It also combines all the things puppies love: running, sniffing, eating, learning and *being with you.*

🐾 Rather than producing your hand at the same level all the time, funk it up by producing it up high, down low, between your legs, etc. Keep puppy engaged by keeping them guessing as to where the hand will appear next!

---

### ○ CASE STUDY: 99 Problems

True story. Waaaaay back many years ago when I was a kid, I was walking a neighbour's Dalmatian puppy along a narrow promenade by the seafront. As we happily strolled, we were approached by a family heading towards us. One of the children in the family, a boy aged around five, was wrestling but certainly getting the better of an ice cream big enough to choke a donkey. You guessed it, as the boy passed us, and without breaking her stride, the puppy shot out a tongue that would

---

make a salamander proud and slurped around four-fifths of the ice cream clean out of the cone! I'm not proud, dear Reader, but me and puppy kept on walking, no one but the boy had noticed, and when I finally mustered the courage to look back from about 30 metres away, the poor kid was stood there, empty cone in hand, looking like the Statue of Liberty had just been shown a card trick!

## CHAPTER 17

# THE TROUBLE WITH 'LEAVE'

The way you're training puppy is by employing what is known in dog training circles as 'Operant Conditioning'. You're asking for a behaviour, and then positively reinforcing that particular behaviour in order for it to become more fluent and reliable in the future.

That's a really clean and efficient way for you to teach and for puppy to learn. No fallout, no dodgy side effects and every delivery of that positive reinforcement comes with a bonus track of positive associations to you, the environment and training in general, all of which are sound investments for your relationship.

So, what about 'Leave'? The problem with using a 'Leave' cue, is that it doesn't teach puppy what you actually want them to *do*. 'Leave' tends to be a go-to instruction that us humans will attempt to use with our puppies, but think about it, it's not really a clear instruction of what to do. Unfortunately, I see it used more as a threat. As always, the most productive tactic will be to ask puppy to do the behaviours that you actually *do* want, instead of trying an ambiguous concept, such as leave. Imagine if I burst into your house now and said 'Leave!' – it could mean a million different things, and we're the same species speaking the same language! As I said earlier in this book, 'leave' doesn't past the Dead Dog Test, namely, if a dead dog can do it, it's not a behaviour! (see page 93)

## SCENARIO ONE

Imagine going into a room that has a teacher in it and 100 chairs laid out. The chairs are numbered 1 to 100. The teacher doesn't want you to sit in any of the chairs numbered 1 to 99. Each time you go to sit, the teacher says 'No!', 'Wrong!', 'Leave it!', 'Off!', 'Incorrect!', etc.

Here's the potential fallout:

- You'll be very confused.
- You'll become frustrated.
- The teacher will become frustrated.
- You'll lose motivation.
- You'll learn the teacher is nothing but bad news.

* You won't enjoy being in the room, or with the teacher.

* Ultimately, if you really want to sit down, you'll learn to ignore the teacher. You'll sit down and therefore be reinforced (by the comfort of sitting) for doing exactly the behaviour the teacher doesn't want you to do!

## SCENARIO TWO

Imagine going into a room that has a teacher in it and 100 chairs laid out. The chairs are numbered 1 to 100. The teacher doesn't want you to sit in any of the chairs numbered 1 to 99. So, they ask you to sit in chair number 100. When you sit in chair number 100, they give you a bar of your favourite chocolate. Get in!

Here's the potential consequences:

* You LOVE this teacher!

* Tomorrow, you'd love the opportunity sit on chair number 100 again please and thank you!

* Teacher's happy.

* You're happy.

* You haven't touched chairs 1 to 99.

We're back to our mutually exclusive behaviours. It's *far* more effective to ask puppy what you *do* want them to do, as opposed to using negative interrupters such as, 'Leave it' or 'No!', *which* never actually tell puppy what you *do* want. At best, 'Leave it' or 'No!' will leave them in limbo; at worst it will damage your relationship.

When I visit clients, I'll often draw a line straight down the middle of a page and I'll ask them to complete the column on the left-hand side which I title, 'What You Don't Want Puppy to Do'.

The page will look something like this:

| What You Don't Want Puppy to Do? | |
|---|---|
| 1) Jump up at visitors | |
| 2) Pull me over to other dogs | |
| 3) Pick up rubbish at the park | |
| 4) 'Steal' dropped items in the kitchen | |

I'll then work through the column on the right-hand side which I'll title 'What Do You Want Instead?' I'll be honest, this is how it normally goes...

Let's say the issue is 'Picking up rubbish at the park'. I'll say to the client, 'Cool, what do you want puppy to do instead?'

They'll invariably reply, 'I want him to *not* pick up rubbish at the park!'

'Not' isn't a behaviour!

We'll chat it through and the client then comes up with the behaviour they *do* want in each case.

The column will now take shape as below:

| What You Don't Want Puppy to Do? | What Do You Want Instead? |
| --- | --- |
| 1) Jump up at visitors | Sit to say 'Hi' |
| 2) Pull me over to other dogs | Look to me when on-lead |
| 3) Pick up rubbish at the park | Run to me when I call him |
| 4) 'Steal' dropped items in the kitchen | Come to me for a nose target |

*Now* we have a training plan:

🐾 Teach 'Sit' like a rock star!

🐾 Teach 'Eye Contact' or 'Reflex To Name' like your life depended on it!

🐾 Teach a 'Total Recall'!

🐾 Teach a 'Nose Target' not to be sniffed at!

You *will* come across the odd (very odd) dog trainer or part-time whisperer down the park who will say, 'Ah, but I taught my dog to "Leave" in class and when I dropped the paracetamol on the kitchen floor and said "Leave!", my dog did.' (Note to self: why does everyone give 'dropped paracetamol' as an example of teaching 'Leave', like they're some kind of clumsy Edward Scissorhands with a banging hangover?)

My thoughts on this 'expert advice' are:

- I bet how they said 'Leave' in class is not how they roared 'LEAVE IT!' when in the emergency situation at home. I'm sure their dog just got the fright of their life and froze. Not good for the pup's relationship to you or their associations with the kitchen.

- When I ask these trainers, 'What does "Leave" mean to your dog?', they'll reply along the lines of, 'Don't touch this,' or 'Don't do that'. Who's to say the puppy's *this* or *that* is the same as your *this* or *that*? Too vague.

- While we're at it, to 'Don't touch' or 'Don't do' is not a behaviour, therefore we cannot teach it and put it on cue. So there!

So, in an ideal world (and living with a puppy *is* an ideal world!), you're going to practise and reinforce those mutually exclusive behaviours so you and puppy will always know exactly what you want them to do.

## TO THE FRIDGE!

However, sometimes the 'sit hits the fan' and you'll need an emergency 'get out of jail card'.

Here it is…

Let's say for some reason you've not had a chance yet to perfect puppy's recall, nose touch or sit. I'm going to give you an exercise that will snap puppy out of whatever mischief they're contemplating and enable you to get them away from potential danger, such as someone leaving the front door open or puppy grabbing the remote control for the TV. It's called, 'To the Fridge'! We need a cue that puppy will react to instantly, similar to the way you're teaching 'Reflex To Name' on page 167.

This is a fun one to teach!

Make sure you have a rich supply of the very, *VERY* best food for puppy in the fridge: fresh chicken, cheese, frankfurters. Whatever floats puppy's boat the most. Now, sit on your settee in your sitting room with puppy milling about and relax … leave it a few minutes then suddenly shout in a happy and excited voice 'TO THE FRIDGE!' and then immediately run to the fridge (obviously). Trust me, puppy will follow, and when you arrive there, open the door and excitedly toss the treats to puppy like a pirate running treasure through their fingers. 'We're rich, rich, I tells yar!'

After 20 seconds of this high-calorie bedlam, stop, go silent and return to your settee like nothing has happened.

Puppy will think, *I've no idea what just went on, but I like it!*

Leave it another five minutes or so and repeat, 'TO THE FRIDGE!' again, run to the kitchen with puppy and have your 30-second Scooby Snack Mardi Gras.

Do this a few times a day, at different times of the day and very soon you'll see how puppy drops *everything* when they hear the beautiful 'To the Fridge!' siren. Don't always do it from the settee. Sometimes announce the exciting news from upstairs, sometimes from the garden. We want 'To the Fridge' to equal *PARTYYYYY!* and for those words to be the common denominators, not the settee.

Once you see evidence of what a lab assistant with 50 pens in their top pocket would call a 'Positive Conditioned Emotional Response' (+CER – namely, you see puppy excited in anticipation when they hear the 'To The Fridge' claxon), you'll then have your emergency protocol to get puppy out of trouble in a positive, exciting way, rather than a suppressive, threatening manner.

And while I'm at it, ponder on this one… 'No' may well be the most overused word in puppy training, yet it probably has the least specific meaning to a puppy!

Something about human nature in there, methinks.

Simply put, do this:

🐾 Control and manage the environment so errors don't occur.

🐾 Reinforce heavily the behaviours you *do* want.

🐾 Take 'Leave' and 'No' out of your puppy training vocabulary.

## SAFE SWAPS

*Going all out for the win!*

You're not gonna believe this but sometimes, just sometimes, puppy *may* pick something up in their mouth that you're not going to want them to have! You've just read in 'The Trouble With Leave' that we always want to ask for the behaviours we 'do' want puppy to do, as opposed to trying to ask for the absence of a behaviour that we don't.

Here I'm going to introduce you to the power of the 'Out!' command and, as with all training, it's a great opportunity for us to keep in the front and centre in our mind, *What does the word mean ... not to us, but to Puppy?*

To your puppy, when they hear you say 'Out!' I want them to have a super-happy reflex-like emotional response that tells them, *Yahoo! Something amazing is coming from Monkey NOW!*

No matter what they're holding, their impulse needs to be to spit it out of their mouth, in anticipation of something even better. Sounds good?

Let's get to it then:

1. Start by sitting with puppy in a nice quiet room with minimal distractions. After a few minutes break the silence by saying 'Out!', count half a second *then* place a fab treat on the floor for pup. The half-second beat between the word and the delivery of the treat will help puppy register what 'Out' *predicts*.

2. Stay silent for a few seconds and repeat randomly, sometimes with a five-second interval between repetitions, sometimes one second, sometimes ten seconds. N.B. the reason we start with no articles in puppy's mouth is because we want to create a super-positive emotional response to hearing the phrase 'Out!' I don't want 'Out!' to mean, 'I'm going to take that away from you' (Boo Hiss!); rather, I want 'Out!' to mean, 'You're gonna get something AWESOME!' Once that emotional response is keyed in, the rest will fall into place. It's therefore very important to condition a *value* to the word

*first*, before ever expecting puppy to understand what you want them to do when they hear it. If, on the first session, puppy has a toy in their mouth and we keep saying, 'Out' before we've even taught puppy what it means, then we're going to get into conflict with our puppy, cause confusion and poison the cue from day one. For us to give a cue and expect a decent response before we've even taught puppy what that the cue means is crazy. It's like you shouting at me, 'SPEAK GREEK! SPEAK GREEK!' I'd be like, 'Tell me a Greek word first, teach me what it means, *then* ask me to speak it. Weirdo.'

3. Do the above for a few short three-minute sessions throughout the day, then for your next session put yourself in the same spot with puppy and introduce a nice boring item, such as a piece of hosepipe or a small block of wood. Kneel on the floor with both hands behind your back, one holding the boring article and one holding the treat. Bring the article around to the front and as soon as puppy shows any interest, even just to look at the item, simply say 'Out!' and bring the exciting treat around front and place on the floor for puppy. While puppy is eating the

treat, place the article back behind your back ready for the next repetition.

4. Next step is to make the 'boring' item marginally less boring by adding slight movement to it as you present it to puppy to investigate; allow puppy to investigate slightly longer, maybe even letting them gently place their mouth on it, but as soon as they do you say 'Out!', hold the article still and then produce the treat as before.

Over time, gradually introduce more and more interesting articles into the training programme. Perhaps upgrade the hosepipe to a knotted tea towel. Increase the intensity, movement and duration of the game with puppy and, as always, make sure you freeze and hold the article stationary, before saying 'Out'.

When you and puppy have become 'Out Masters', you can then introduce the 'Out!' into your play sessions (see page 143 on 'Play'), which will help you develop further games such as fetch.

Funk it up by having two identical tuggy toys behind your back, introduce one out front and let the play begin; when you both have hold of the toy, suddenly freeze, say 'Out!' then immediately introduce the second toy in an animated way for puppy to latch on to.

Luckily the 'grass is always greener on the other side' for puppies and they really subscribe to 'the-active-bird-not-in-the-mouth is better than the-dormant-bird-in-the-mouth', so it's really important that the toy you want puppy to let go of must always become boring *before* you give the cue 'Out!' Make it boring by stopping all movement and tension. That way puppy will always spit out the 'dormant bird' in anticipation of the 'active bird'.

In my experience, this is by far the best way to teach puppy to let go of something in their mouth. I've used it with thousands of dogs and it was also my go-to training method for teaching security dogs to let go of bad guys. Believe me, these dogs *really* wanted to hold on to what was clenched between their teeth (and so did the bad guys!); if it worked for them, it'll work for you!

So, there you have it, *THE* best way to get puppy to drop an item.

If, however, you've not had a chance to teach 'Out' properly yet or you get caught unawares one day when puppy appears around the corner doing an impression of Jack Sparrow with a cutlass between his teeth, remember, you've always got your emergency 'TO THE FRIDGE!' to call upon.

CHAPTER 18

# THE RUCKSACK WALK

## (OR 'WHY DOGS DON'T RUN IN PERU!')

One of the many great things I get to do in my job as a dog behaviour lecturer is travel. As well as lecturing, I also travel on fact-finding missions to ensure my teaching is 'on-point'. I go to South Africa to consult at a Pitbull sanctuary in Johannesburg, visit Bahrain to develop detection dog training and, on a recent teaching trip to Australia, was lucky enough to explore the world of herding dogs in Perth.

However, it's deepest, darkest Peru that I want to speak to you about now...

In modern dog training, a lot of emphasis is given to allowing the dog to have a choice: the choice to make the right decisions or the choice to say 'No' if they are feeling uncomfortable. Basically, the thinking is to never put the dog under any physical or mental pressure to do as we desire.

However, I often wonder, given the *choice*, what *exactly* would a domestic dog choose to do? As soon as we have a dog in a room with four walls or we pop a lead and harness onto the dog, surely a lot of their natural options of choice are limited?

That's where Peru comes in!

I had heard of the street dogs in Cuzco, Peru.

Now, these dogs are 'owned', but not in the usual Westernised way. Basically, from 6am each day, the dogs are turned out from the home by their owners and they hook up with their other doggie buddies and spend the day getting up to *exactly what they choose to do*. At 10–11pm, you see them all return to their respective doorways, the doors open, the dogs get their B&B and tomorrow the adventure continues.

On one particular trip, after I landed at Cuzco airport, the taxi driver (who was wearing two hats, I didn't question), asked me what I did for a living. Once he knew I was a dog trainer he said, 'You'll love the city centre, mi amigo, all of the dogs stop and wait for the traffic lights to go red before crossing the road.'

Sure they do. I've just come down in an airplane, mate, not the last shower.

Fast-forward 30 minutes and there we are, pulling up to the traffic lights in heavy traffic. To our left are about a dozen dogs of all shapes and sizes waiting patiently for the red light to *beep beep beep*, signalling that it's safe to cross!

The signal changes and over they cross, no rush, like a cartoon canine parade. Super-cool.

A perfect combination of how animals learn and natural selection right there. And I hadn't even unpacked my bags!

So that was me for the next wonderful two weeks: video camera in hand, I'd follow hundreds of these dogs, sometimes solitary, sometimes in loosely formed social groups to see exactly what they got up to. Here's some things they *didn't* get up to:

- They rarely ran. No rush, time was always on their side. They showed no signs of panic to desperately get to any particular location.

- They rarely barked. No real elements of arousal or conflict.

- They never chased birds, paper bags or tennis balls!

In the middle of Cuzco is Plaza De Armas, a large pedestrian area surrounded by public gardens and fountains marking the colonial centre of the city. On one particularly nice day (and they're all nice days in the high altitude of Cuzco, as long as you've got lungs the size of a squirrel's purse), up to 500 people can be seen mooching around the square, having a coffee or just sitting on the grass enjoying the view (or gasping for breath!). In addition to the 500 or so people, you'll see 150–200 dogs also mooching around, sunbathing or just generally hanging out. Doing exactly as they *choose*.

So, given the choice, what did the dogs of Cuzco choose to do:

- 🐾 *Touch*: they liked to 'be' with people. I photographed a young couple sat by a foundation; a large mixed-breed was laid alongside them. Not fussing them, just lying there, with his flank touching the leg of one of the unknown strangers.

- 🐾 *Smell*: they liked to investigate any new smell. Discarded boxes, bins, even a mislaid child's teddy bear were all subjected to a good old olfactory once-over.

- 🐾 *Be curious*: given the opportunity, novel items such as handbags were all scanned with the intensity of a newly promoted customs official.

- 🐾 *Eat*: of course! Any free pickings were gratefully received.

- 🐾 *Watch*: just be still, relax and watch the world go by.

These dogs were happy, relaxed and fulfilled. This got me to thinking: *How can I deliver similar to the dogs 'back home'?*

So far, a lot of what I've written in this book is basically how to 'get' your puppy to do a, b and c or how to 'stop' them doing x, y and z.

I don't want all of your time with puppy to be purely contingent on behaviours or focused on control and management. Those factors are great when it comes to getting the behaviour we want or to keep puppy safe and out of trouble, but surely there's more to life than that, eh? This is where the Rucksack Walk comes in.

The Rucksack Walk is something I developed years ago for dogs and people of all ages, as a way to enjoy spending time together in a pressure-free, performance-free and safe way. If you have dog that likes hanging out with you, 90% of your problems are gone.

In all honesty, the Rucksack Walk was born out of necessity. My work is not only with fresh-faced, excitable puppies but with geriatric dogs, nervous dogs, injured dogs, rescue dogs, dogs in rescue kennels, dogs that 'work' for a living, dogs on restricted exercise, dogs that need space, dogs that don't cope well with strangers, or dogs that have been labelled 'reactive', 'aggressive' or 'shy'. I also deal with owners that have limited time, limited locations and/or limited mobility. I deal with operational dog handlers who have come off a 10-hour stressful shift with their security or detection dog. When do dogs and people get time to decompress? Walking your puppy is not about clocking up miles, it really ain't.

As a result of seeing so many dogs that needed exploratory and bonding opportunities and so many owners that were pushed for time, I decided to come up with an activity that didn't demand a high level of training but ticked similar boxes to those being enjoyed by the super-satisfied dogs of Peru. An activity that invested in the dog/owner relationship and gave the dog the mental 'release' they so desire for a fulfilled life. Notice I refer to mental *release* as opposed to the more commonly used mental *stimulation*. Stimulation implies excitement, arousal and raising the levels of nervous activity in the body. I see a lot of pups that suffer because they're conditioned to approach everything they see in the outside world with such a high level of arousal. That arousal can then get puppy and you into trouble, as they feel the need to hit everything at 100mph, not waiting to think, reason or weigh up the options before rushing in – often leaving you behind!

I'm all for games and fun with puppy. It's one of my great pleasures in life. But not *always*. A good friend should be someone you're happy just to be 'with'.

That being said, I want you to be able to give puppy a ton of what they need: recall, loose lead walking, focus, adventure, exploration, olfactory satisfaction, food(!), novelty and a nice fat dose of serotonin (the 'feel good' neurotransmitter) and oxytocin (the bonding or 'love' hormone), *without* the presence of an adrenalin rush.

'It can't be done,' you cry.

Don't cry.

Read on.

## THE RUCKSACK WALK: THE TOOLS YOU WILL NEED

For your rucksack walk you'll need:

- 🐾 A rucksack (funnily enough!)

- 🐾 A long line (five metres or so)

- 🐾 A comfortable puppy harness

- 🐾 Fully loaded treat pouch

- 🐾 A puppy chew

- 🐾 A 'thing' (anything here will do, as long as it's safe for puppy to investigate, e.g. a hairbrush, a book, a comb, a shoe ... all will be revealed!)

- 🐾 A Tupperware box, containing a novel scent (again, anything here as long as it's safe for puppy to sniff, e.g. a teabag, a used sock, catnip, etc)

- 🐾 Another Tupperware box, containing a novel food (grab something safe from the fridge that puppy has never had before)

🐾 Fifteen minutes. If you can't grab 15 minutes well ... you can!

## THE RUCKSACK WALK: THE RULES

I originally didn't want any rules in the Rucksack Walk as by definition I wanted it to be as relaxed as possible; however, therein anarchy lies! With that in mind:

Rule No. 1: Do not see this SOLELY as a 'training' exercise – SEE IT AS A BONDING OPPORTUNITY.
Rule No. 2: Every word is a *whisper*.
Rule No. 3: Treat everything that comes from the rucksack as if it were a baby bird.

So here goes, your first Rucksack Walk with puppy. 'citing!

Drive to your location with puppy, ideally somewhere quiet and reasonably close. Put on your treat pouch and attach the long line to puppy's harness. Unload puppy from your car and make sure all of your interactions are relaxed and quiet. We're using the long line here for safety and we're keeping everything relaxed and quiet to minimise arousal. It's going to take a few repetitions before you and puppy get into the groove of moving slowly outside but once you do, it's a real lightbulb moment.

I see so many owners walk their dogs in a real, 'Ready,

steady, kick the front door down and GO GO GO!' then speed around the block with puppy because they've got to be back in a certain amount of time and need to cover a certain amount of distance ... etc.

No!

Those kind of walks become so high-octane that puppy is conditioned to grab at as much information as possible before the walk comes to an abrupt halt. That's when we see the urgent pulling to get to all the sniffs, the desperate attempts to gather as much information as possible before the shutters come down as quick as they went up.

That's no fun.

That's stressful.

Imagine you're at a restaurant with a colleague, say one of those swanky sushi places where the food slowly rotates around the tables on a conveyor belt as you chat. Now, imagine you're famished, but the conveyor belt is going around far too fast. You're going to desperately grab at the food as it goes by, you're not going to fully appreciate the menu and you're certainly not going engage with your dinner guest. Any conversation will be wasted.

A 'quick march' around the block with puppy is the equivalent of the speeding sushi conveyor belt.

Don't do it.

Slow it down.

Remember the dogs of Peru.

## Step 1

'Mooch' to your spot. What I mean by 'mooch' is to stroll, to wander slowly and relaxed to an area maybe five minutes away. No urgency. Compromise with puppy; if they want to walk over to an area to sniff or wee, great. As long as the long line remains slack, go with them. It's important they get to investigate the environment. If the long line goes tight or puppy begins to run, you just slow to a stop. We don't want to allow urgency or tension to sneak into our Rucksack Walk. When the lead goes back to being slack, continue your mooch.

Here's some sneaky training for the control freaks out there!

If, as you mooch, puppy glances towards you, say 'Good' and slowly throw a treat out to the opposite side of you that puppy is on. I've just written that myself and even I don't get it so I'll try again...

Imagine puppy is off to your left having a sniff, they're three metres away, the long line is slack so you patiently wait. If they happen to look to you, say 'Good', to mark the behaviour, and toss a treat out to your right. Puppy will then run 'through' you to get the treat.

The beauty of this method is:

🐾 You're 'capturing' the checking in by reinforcing it with the treat.

As a by-product, puppy is also feeling good about doing a recall to you on their way to the treat.

 You're not 'competing' with the environment, because they're getting the treat *and* a new area to explore on the other side of you.

Three for the price of one!

If puppy doesn't check in with you, don't sweat it. It's just information for you that they need to investigate the location further. Tomorrow's another day, the more comfortable they become in the environment, the more they'll permit themselves to be able to check in with you. Be poised to 'mark' and reinforce it with a treat when they do.

## Step 2

When you get to your desired location, you're going to do a few recall circuits as discussed in our 'Recall' chapter (see page 197).

Here is the only place on your Rucksack Walk that you're allowed to speak louder than a whisper. Get it out of your system because it's all hush-hush after this! Keep the triangle layout for your recalls nice and small, with sides shorter than the length of your long line, to ensure you can maintain contact with puppy at all times if required.

I want you to stick to circuit recalls, as the triangle will ensure you're going over the same area time and time again. This familiarity of terrain will ensure your recalls are not having to compete with conflicting novel smells on the ground.

Once you're done, sit down and both hit the deck!

## Step 3

Don't you just love sitting on the ground outside with your puppy? (if you haven't done it yet, then that's another reason why you need the Rucksack Walk in your life!). When I teach group classes, I love seeing the owners smile when I ask them to all relax and sit down on the grass with their puppies. I'm sure it's a link back to our nursery school days when the teacher said on a Friday afternoon, 'You've all been so good this week, we'll have our story outside.'

*OUTSIDE!? Be still my beating heart!*

So, sit down with puppy; you've both just had a good run doing your circuit recalls so you're ready to take a breather.

Now we're going to introduce our Tupperware Novel Scent.

*NOT SO FAST!*

Remember, everything that comes out of the rucksack is a baby bird. Be slow and curious in your movements. You're the *best* children's entertainer hired to pull the *best* magic tricks out of that rucksack.

As you ever-so-slowly begin to unzip the bag, whisper to yourself and puppy, 'Oh my, what's this?'

N.B. this is not any old, 'Oh my, what's this?'

This is a Marks & Spencer, '*Oh ... My ... Wh ... What's ... This!?*' that takes an edge-of-the-seat 10 seconds to whisper.

Slowly take the box from the rucksack, shielding it gently in your hands like the baby bird that it is. I defy any puppy to not put their nose in and say, 'Seriously, mate, what is it?'

Enjoy and elongate that conversation.

This is a great opportunity for you to practise your connection with puppy. We know from Peru that pups love to be 'with' you, they love to investigate scent. Here's your opportunity to share. So slowly, delicately and deliberately open the very slightest edge of the box, allow puppy to sniff, then close the box once more. Lift it up. Bring it back down again and allow puppy to investigate another tiny little bit. You hold the box all the time. It's for you and puppy to investigate *together*.

A couple of minutes. That's enough. PUPPY HAS EXPERIENCED THE SCENT – NO NEED TO GIVE THEM THE SCENT ITEM – so then slowly close the box, unzip the rucksack, put the precious treasure back in and close the rucksack.

*But's what's this, Mum's unzipping the rucksack again,* OMG, OMG, OMG, *shut up ... What's coming next?*

## Step 4

As promised earlier ... it's the 'Thing'!

Again, slow, curious movements from you. It could be a baby bird, it could be an unexploded bomb, either way, softly, softly does it and remember: nothing more than a whisper.

Let's say you've pulled a comb from the rucksack.

Dogs in Peru love to investigate novel items; your puppy's the same.

Initially, keep it shrouded in your hands, then run your finger slowly over the teeth to make strange rattling sounds. Maybe hold it to your lips and blow softly, what noise does that make? Let puppy sniff, feel and slowly explore the comb, inch by inch before it delicately (remember the baby bird/unexploded bomb!) gets placed back into the rucksack.

## Step 5

Intro the big one.

Bring out the Novelty Food Box. Now, this is a *BIG* deal for puppy, so embrace it. Why just feed it to puppy in two seconds when your baby bird approach will allow you both to connect and take pleasure in the ceremony for two *minutes*?

What's going to have more value?

What's going to connect the two of you best?

When the food has been eaten, slowly, *slowly* put the box back in the rucksack and then produce, with Svengali-like orchestration from elsewhere in the rucksack, the Chew.

By passively touching puppy as they chew, you're giving puppy's brain the opportunity to release all of those feel-good chemicals such as serotonin, dopamine and oxytocin. Combined with the touch, you'll be creating a real love-in and decreasing stress in both parties!

## Step 6

When you're done – and remember there's no rush – pop the chew back in the rucksack, pick up your long line and get ready to mooch back to your car. I want you to *slowly* mooch back to your car along the same route as you came in; that way you're not going to be going over new, distracting smells.

This time, as you head back, when puppy checks in with you say 'Good!' but rather than throwing the treat to your other side, reward puppy next to your leg as you continue to walk.

Because you're going over the same ground and you've just spent a wonderful 15 minutes in each other's company, puppy won't need to urgently explore and investigate the environment as much as when you first arrived. By reinforcing next to your leg, guess what: you're training loose lead walking for free!

When you're back at the car, secure puppy safely in your vehicle and head off home knowing that you've had a quality experience that has added to your lifelong relationship with puppy.

Not bad for 15 minutes.

## Important Considerations

- It's only 15 minutes.

- Stay off your phone!

- Maybe substitute one of puppy's 'normal' daily walks with a Rucksack Walk. After a week, see how you both feel. (I'm guessing a little more Zen than usual!)

- A Rucksack Walk is great for staying out of the way of other dogs!

- Great for small spaces.

- Great for nervous puppies.

- A great way to chill adrenalin-junkie puppies.

- A great way for *you* to decompress after a stressful day.

- Enjoy!

Back in Peru, I would sit with the dogs as the sun went

down and ponder on the wonderful opportunities they get making their own life choices, day in, day out. One of them, a large female mastiff-type dog, sat still watching a dandelion floating for a full five minutes and I thought how lucky she was to be just living in the moment. I then realised I myself had therefore been watching her for a full five minutes...

For any creature in the animal kingdom, us included, to have such life choices is a real gift.

With a Rucksack Walk, it's a gift you're now able to give puppy and, in return, receive.

# CHAPTER 19

# PUPPY SCHOOL, GROUP CLASSES AND VETS, OH MY!

Yaaaaaaaaaaaaaaaaaaaaaaaaaaaaaaay!
Or Nay?

Now you know my backstory, you know how much I *loved* dog classes when I was a kid; well, the freaky dog boy in me is still as passionate today as that kid was back then. However, I'm also far more aware of the good, the bad and the ugly of dog training classes, so here's a few tips to guide you through the maze.

What I wanted back then in my puppy classes is what I want for you and your puppy now. A great puppy class and trainer can be so beneficial: you and puppy will get to make new friends, you'll have a professional you can trust to 'hold your hand' throughout all the puppy development stages and you'll fine tune the training that you and puppy will need for life. Puppy should also get to make friends in a controlled and safe environment. Ultimately, puppy will learn that dogs are cool, people are cool and you're super-cool!

A poor puppy class can be so detrimental. Just because they say they're a professional dog trainer, don't assume they're a *good* professional dog trainer. Remember, Sweeney Todd was a professional barber!

Ask around, get personal recommendations and if something doesn't feel right then move on, it's a buyer's market and it's too important not to get right. When you first make contact with the trainer, don't be afraid of giving them a grilling! When I teach classes, I love to know that my owners want the best for their puppies. If all owners showed such ambition and commanded a high standard of their trainers from the start, then the quality of puppy training services would only improve.

Here's a list of things your puppy class *must* offer:

- An experienced, friendly and qualified trainer. Look for qualifications with recognised bodies such as the Institute of Modern Dog Trainers – my organisation puts their trainers through a rigorous assessment process to ensure quality.

- Sufficient space so all the class can spread out and find more room if required. *No more* than six to eight pups per trainer.

- Lots of opportunity to ask questions about your own puppy.

- The opportunity to contact your trainer out of class if necessary.

- Constructive, pressure-free exercises. The trainer must let you know the benefit of each exercise and technique. If you cannot see the benefit of an exercise, you won't commit to it!

- A 100% *rejection* of any harsh, punitive or aversive methods.

- An alternative behaviour for you to reinforce in place of any unwanted behaviours.

- Fun! If you don't look forward to going to class with puppy, find another class. Neurological science tells us that you (and puppy) will learn much better if you're having fun.

- Training with only comfortable, cruelty-free equipment. No choke chains, slip leads, pinch collars – *no exceptions*.

- Learning. You and puppy should learn something new *every week*.

I'm not one to dwell on the negatives, but dog trainers can be an odd bunch (present company excepted, obvs!).

As I said earlier, they can sometimes get wrapped up in believing they're the king or queen of the village hall between 7pm and 8pm on a Thursday night and can slip into becoming a pseudo-sergeant major complete with a wolf-print fleece uniform and matching baseball cap.

As a kid, I witnessed a trainer saying to an owner in puppy class, 'How can we expect our pup to listen, when *you* can't even listen yourself!' Man alive! Even as a kid I knew that was not how to motivate and encourage an owner to do their best for puppy in class. If that was the limit of their teaching skills, what hope was there for the pups? That evening I decided, *I'm going to be a dog trainer when I grow up.*

In addition to standard puppy classes, you may well have seen 'puppy parties' advertised. Puppy parties are often hosted at veterinary clinics and are for puppies that have not yet had their full vaccinations. Again, puppy parties can be great, or they can suck.

A puppy party *should not* be an opportunity for all the pups to run around off-lead bashing into each other while the vet nurse discusses how to clean your dog's ears and brush their teeth. Out of six pups there, three may be having a wonderful time, two may be hiding under a chair learning that other dogs are scary, and one may be learning that the only way to tell a pup to back off is to snap at them. The risk/benefit of 'all off-lead' is just not worth it.

Off-lead interaction, done properly, can be fun and beneficial.

Rather than a free-for-all, it should look more like two well-matched pups off-lead at the same time: as the two pups interact, the trainer should be commenting to everyone on observable body language (which you're now an expert on having read the Body Language chapter! #There'sATestAtTheEnd!).

The trainer should also be encouraging each owner to step in on a regular basis to ensure the pup-to-pup interaction does not descend into a crescendo of arousal. The play should remain friendly and serve as an opportunity to create positive memories for all.

Here's the coup, find a trainer that teaches you to work *with* puppy, not against them. Find a puppy school that sets a tone to enable you to teach puppy exactly the way you'd love to be taught yourself.

# GOODBYE, AND GOOD LUCK

So, I guess this is where we go our separate ways. You're going to have so much fun and develop lifelong memories for each other. It's exciting times and I've got to be honest, I'm a little envious! Take care of puppy and remember there's no such thing as a 'bad' training session, merely information on how to plan and deliver your next one. Set yourselves up for success, aim for achievable criteria, and spend your living hours looking for the puppy behaviours you want more of, then reinforce them like the dog training Ninja you've now become!

Training a puppy is a process, not an event.

Build an optimistic puppy and enjoy your journey.

Good luck.

Steve Mann

# ACKNOWLEDGEMENTS

....Oh hello!

Still here?

I didn't think anyone ever read the acknowledgements yet here you are, sat watching the credits role while everyone else turns on their phone and dusts popcorn off their laps...

Well, let my very first thanks go to *you*, Dear Reader. Thanks for taking the time to read my book, I really hope you enjoyed it.

Huge thanks to my wife Gina for constantly fanning the flames of my passion for dogs and for never insisting I ever get a 'real' job. To our son Luke, who has an empathy for animals that is second to none. So proud.

You're still here? Righto...

Team IMDT, your work to develop education and support for dog trainers and behaviourists worldwide is phenomenal, and a special mention needs to go to Alison Martin, a golden cog in the IMDT machine.

To Martin Roach, who emailed me after seeing me on the *Lorraine* show and suggested I write a book – obviously address all complaints to him! Thanks, Mart, for holding my hand throughout the whole writing process, it's been an honour working with someone who has the same taste as me in music and fashion, and the same forced taste as me in hairstyles...

Thanks to Blink Publishing, particularly Beth and Matt, for making *Easy Peasy Puppy Squeezy* actually happen. As a kid I would ravenously read dog training books from cover to cover and fantasise about how cool it would be to actually write one! I'll be honest, it's pretty cool!

Now, I know you don't even know my family, but if you're still game...

Mum and Dad, thank you for teaching me to do lots of what I love. I'm still getting away with it. Hurrah! To Anthony and Maria, my brother and sister, thank you for being such good kids when we were growing up, which in turn gave me plenty of elbow room to sneak away to play with dogs!

Finally...

Thank you to all of our dogs, past, present and future, without whom this book could never have been written, and to Pablo my staffie, without whom this book would've been written at least 6 months earlier!

# INDEX

alternative behaviour 46
American Kennel Club 51
Angus (dog) 182–3
Animal Behaviour and Husbandry
1, 11
animal welfare 33
anthropomorphism 73
anti-dog-trainer method 193–5
antler horns 32
ants-in-their-pants 160
appropriate action 99
arousal, learning inhibited by 99
artificial additives and preservatives
33, 34–5
Ash (dog) 2
association 30, 36, 161–2
automatic sit 89–90

backing away 71
Bailey (dog) 206–7
basic sit 82
bat-ears 72
beach dogs 75

bedroom 42–3
bedtime routine 31, 42
behaviour machine 45
behavioural science 1, 11, 18
Big Dave (dog) 162–6
biodegradable bags 35
biting 97, 98–100
bladder control 52
Blessed, Brian 171–2, 173–4
blinking 70, 123
body language 7, 47, 54, 61, 66,
74–6
  common signals 68
  raised hackles 76
  rocking horse 77
  rules of reading 67–8
  stress 79
body-slamming 119
Bolster, Geert De 38
bonding 147, 236
bowls 26, 30, 31
bull's pizzles 32

cables 40, 102
call to action 79
Canine Holy Grail 134
captured behaviour 204
Carlos Fandangos of the West (dog) 2, 43–4
carpets 102
case studies 61–3, 91–5, 108–10, 162–6, 168, 171–4, 182–3, 196, 206–7, 213–14
cats 47, 85
chemicals 40
chewing 16–17, 31, 33, 39, 40, 97, 100–3, 105
chewing remedy 102–3
chews 26, 30, 32, 39, 40, 102, 103, 109–10
child-gates 54
children 143–4, 213–14
choke hazards 40
Chump (dog) 172
circling 55
Clary, Julian 171
cleaning up 26, 35–6, 54, 58
closed mouth 71, 79
Colin (dog) 168–71
collar 26, 36–7
comfort blanket 25, 26–7, 30, 31, 41, 42–3
comfortable harness 26, 37–8
commands v. cues 83
common sense 22, 24, 33
common signals 68
conditioning 107
conducive environment 54, 55
confidence building 60
conflict 47
consistency 47
constant stare 69
context, understanding 67, 77

control and management 22–4
Control of Dogs Order (1992) 37
counter-conditioning 127–8
crescent approach 75
crossbreeds 2, 9
crouched back 123
Crufts 20
cues 83, 86–7, 177, 215–16

Darwin, Charles 80
Dead Dog Test 93, 216
den training 27
Den Wizard 30, 103
dens 25, 27–30, 31, 41–2, 54, 55, 59
dependence 97
desensitisation 122–4
designated watchers 54
detection dogs 11
diary-keeping 58
Diesel (dog) 91–5
dilated pupils 69
displacement 77–8, 79
distance 83, 84, 86–7, 192
distraction 83, 84, 85–6, 192–3
diversion techniques 31–2
diverting eyes 69
dog tag 26, 37
Dougal (dog) 172, 173, 174
'download' time 47
Drunk Dog Walking 188–9
duration 83, 84–5, 192

ears 72–3, 79
Einstein, Albert 143
electricity cables 40
emergency recall 205–6
environment exposure table 116
environmental considerations 35, 177

enzymatic cleaner 26, 35–6, 54, 58
erect ears 73
erect tail 72
'escape' routes 120–1
etiquette 131–42
evidence-based learning 15
excitement 16, 17, 52, 53
exploration 31, 102, 120–1
exposure tables 116, 118
*The Expression of the Emotions in Man
and Animals* (Darwin) 80
eye contact 34, 75, 76, 156, 175–83,
186, 186–93 *passim*, 219
eyes, how to read 69–70

fear periods 128–30
feeding 26, 32–3
feet 74
fencing 40
'Fenton' sensation 196
fertiliser 40
fireworks 67
first night 41–3
folded ears 72
frequency 183
'To the Fridge' 221–2, 227
furrowed brow 123
fulcrum recalls 203–4
funk it up! 83–7, 182, 195, 200–1,
212–13, 226
furniture 40, 44, 46, 102, 103, 106

gardens 39, 40
glassware 40
greeting protocol 165
greeting wees 59–60

hair-standing 76
half-weeing 57
Hamilton, Lewis 17–18

harness 26, 37–8, 121, 132, 168,
185, 187, 188, 190, 199, 230, 235,
236
head tilt 73–4
helicopter tail 72
'Hi', teaching dogs how to say 17
hiding away 124
home, modifications to 39–40
horizontal lip retraction 71
hormones 79
hot-water bottle 26, 31, 41
house soiling *see* toilet training
houseplants 39
*How to Punish Your Puppy* 20

inappropriate action 99
indoor toilet training 52, 56, 58
Institute of Modern Dog Trainers
11, 248
interactive feeders 32, 33
interrupter 104–8
intimidation 106
isolation, avoidance of 12

Jarvis (dog) 61–3
Jones, David 52
jumping up 153–66

Kelly, Lorraine 182, 183
Kennel Club 51
kit list 25–40, 136–8, 235–6
Kongs 32, 34, 102, 109, 157

laid-back ears 79
laws 37
lead-pulling 186
leads 26, 38–9, 137, 140, 185–96
licking 17
Lincoln, Abraham 20
lip licking 123

lip retraction 71
listening skills 65–6, 80
littermates 31, 114
loose leads 185–96
*Lorraine* 182

management and control 22
Mann, Gina (wife) 2
Mann, Luke (son) 2
Mann, Steve 254
  becomes dog trainer 10–11
  early life 5–8
  experience of 1–2
  'Freaky Dog Boy' sobriquet 5, 6, 10, 12
  neighbours' dogs 6, 9
marking 82
Martin and Kaye (friends) 163, 164
'me' time 47
MEB (mutually exclusive behaviour) 23, 155–8, 160, 188
mental release 234
meta signals 78
misconceptions 14, 15, 47
mobile phones 39
mood 106
morning stretch 68
mother dependence 97
motivation 15, 46, 114, 179
mouth 70–1, 97–110
mouth manners 98–100
muscle memory 106–7
mutually exclusive behaviour *see* MEB

Nancy (dog) 2
nappy sacks 35
natural products 33
negativity, avoiding 63
neonatal stage 113

Norton, Graham 206, 207
nose 209–14
nosiness 39
Nylabone 32, 102

off-lead walking 186–7, 250–1
old-school training *see* traditional thinking
online resources 16, 39
orientation reflex 73
other dogs 6, 66, 70, 74, 75, 77, 80, 91–4 *passim*, 131–42 *passim*, 176, 178, 183, 186, 218, 219, 230, 244, 250
outside toilet training 53, 56
overnight toilet training 59

Pablo (dog) 2
pacing 56
pain relief 16, 101
panic, how to avoid 30
panting 79, 123
parks 131–42, 196, 206–7, 218–19
patience 54, 179
Pele (dog) 2
perspective 11, 13, 56, 105, 149
piloerection 76
pinned-back ears 73
plastic 109
play 143–52
play biting 98–100
poisonous plants 39
ponds 40
Poo and Pee Diary 58
poo bags (*see also* toilet training) 26, 35, 54, 140
positive association 30, 34, 36, 56–7, 62, 63, 122, 124–7
positive conditioned emotional response (PCER) 36, 128, 222

positive interrupter 104–8
positive reinforcement 23
primary socialisation 114
proofing 39–40, 85, 88, 180
pseudo-expertise 14
pulled-back ears 73
pulling, on lead 186
punishment:
    consequences of 21
    how to link 18–19
    mistaken belief in 20, 57, 159–
      60, 249
    when to apply 16–17
pupil dilation 69
puppy pens 54
puppy play 144–8
puppy-proofing 39–40, 85, 88, 180
Puppy's Personal Bank 99

quality sleep 47
quick-about-turn 128–9

raised hackles 76
raised paw 74, 123
'read and respond' 66
recall 34, 197–207, 221
recall circuits 201–3
reinforced behaviour 34, 53, 82–3,
  86
reinforcement placement 190–1
relationship building 31
relaxed mouth 70–1
remote controls 39
rescue centres 11
resource guarding 10
restrained recall 199–200
rocking horse 77
rope toys 32, 102
RTN (reflex to name) 167–74
rubber toys 32, 109, 110

rucksack walk 136, 229–45
running 198

safe swaps 223–7
science-based dog training 1, 11, 14,
  20, 249
sclera 70
Scooby Doo 73
Scott, Selina 172
scratching 56, 69, 78
'seasoned' blanket 41, 42–3
secondary socialisation 114
self-grooming 78
sensitivity 128
shoes 39, 103
sights 27, 41, 42, 114, 116, 117, 135
sitting 34, 81–95, 89–90, 112
sitting boss 163
sitting ninja level 87
Skinner, B.F. 18
sleep 47, 55
smells 27, 41, 42, 114, 116, 117, 118,
  120, 126, 232, 240, 243
sniffing 17, 54, 55, 75, 78
socialisation 47, 111–30
soft eyes 69
sounds 27, 28, 41, 42, 69, 114, 116,
  117, 120, 135, 137, 161, 191, 242
speed awareness 18, 21
Spider (dog) 2
squinty eyes 70
staring 69
stimuli exposure table 118
stress 78–80
stretching 68
stubbornness, misconceptions of
  15, 47
submissive urination 52, 60
Summer (dog) 2
supervision 54

survival instinct 10
suspicion, how to avoid 46
symptom and cause, addressing 107–8

table cloths 40
tactile textures 32
tail between legs 72, 123
tails 40, 71–2
teamwork 46
teeth/teething 31, 32, 98, 101, 107
telling-off, avoidance of 100
tenseness 71
texture 27, 32, 34, 109, 110, 114, 116, 117, 118, 126
things exposure table 118
Three Ds 83–8, 192–3
tight mouth 71, 79
toilet training 16, 17, 25, 33, 35, 36, 42, 43, 47, 51, 51–63
  customising 58
  overnight 59
  signs to look out for 55–6
  timing of 53–4
  and treats 56
tongue-flicking 79
total recaller 197–207
tough love 41
toys 26, 30, 31–2, 39, 102, 105, 109, 110
traditional thinking 7–8, 15, 16–17, 57
transitional stage 97, 113
treats 26, 30, 34–5, 41, 56, 62, 82, 99, 105, 137
triangulation 73
triggers 20
trust 80
tugging 148–51
TWOFOHJOT 191

The Underdog Show 1, 171
unwanted behaviour 21
urination see half-weeing; greeting wees; submissive urination; toilet training

V-shaped ears 72
vertical lip retraction 71
vets 247
vibrissae 71
vinegar 36
violence, mistaken belief in 20–1
vizslas 72
vocalising 123

wagging 40, 71–2
Walcott, Theo 91, 93
walking 53, 185–96
water 30, 40
weedkiller 40
weeing see half-weeing; greeting wees; submissive urination; toilet training
wellbeing 80
whale eye 70
'What Hand?' 151–2
whining 43, 56, 79
wide eyes 123

yawning 68–9, 78
Yorkie (dog) 9–10
YouTube 196

Zebedee-Dog 165
zombiedoodle 93